N
W E
S

Iqaluit

CANADIAN SHIELD

NEWFOUNDLAND

Hudson Bay

QUEBEC

HUDSON BAY LOWLANDS

50°N

50°W

St. John's ⊙

LOWLANDS

APPALACHIAN REGION

PRINCE EDWARD ISLAND

NEW BRUNSWICK

Charlottetown ⊙

NOVA SCOTIA

ONTARIO

Quebec City ⊙

Fredericton ⊙

Halifax ⊙

St. Lawrence River

Lake Superior

ST. LAWRENCE

Atlantic Ocean

40°N

Ottawa ★

Toronto

L. Ontario

Lake Michigan

Lake Huron

Lake Erie

0          500 km

80°W       70°W       60°W

90°W

60°W    40°W    20°W

80°N

70°N

# Our Country, Canada

**Mary Cairo**
**Luci Soncin**

DUVAL HOUSE
PUBLISHING

Copyright © 2001 Duval House Publishing Inc.

5 4

Duval House Publishing Inc.
18228 – 102 Avenue
Edmonton, AB T5S 1S7
Ph: (780) 488-1390
Tollfree: 1-800-267-6187
Fax: (780) 482-7213
Website: http://www.duvalhouse.com

## Authors

Mary Cairo and Luci Soncin

National Library of Canada Cataloguing in Publication Data

Cairo, Mary.
 Our country, Canada

Includes index.
ISBN 1-55220-201-1

1. Canada--Juvenile literature.   I. Soncin, Luciana.
II. Title.
FC57.C28 2001          971          C2001-910521-5
F1008.2.C28 2001

Printed and bound in Canada

## Special Thanks

Kara Fry, Grade 4 Teacher, and the staff at the Mundo Peetabeck Education Authority, Fort Albany, Ontario

Murray Gillespie of Winnipeg, Manitoba.

## Validators

*Educational*

Dolores Cascone
Curriculum Resource Teacher
Toronto Catholic District School Board

Betty Goulden
Educational Consultant
Keswick, Ontario

Mary Nelson
Teacher (retired)
Calgary Public Board of Education
Calgary, Alberta

Pat Waters
Curriculum Consultant (retired)
Waterloo Catholic District School Board

*Content*

Dr. Bruce Rains
Department of Earth and Atmospheric Science
University of Alberta
Edmonton, Alberta

*Bias Reviewer*

John Smith
Principal
Green Glade Senior Public School
Mississauga, Ontario

Many website addresses have been identified in this textbook. These are provided as suggestions and are not intended to be a complete resource list. Duval House Publishing does not guarantee that these websites will not change or will continue to exist. Duval House does not endorse the content of the website nor any websites linked to the site. You should consult with your teacher whenever using Internet resources.

We acknowledge the financial support of the Government of Canada through the Book Publishing Industry Development Program (BPIDP) for our publishing activities.

Canada

## Acknowledgements

The authors would like to acknowledge those involved in the production of the book. We are grateful to Karen Iversen of Duval House Publishing for her vision and guidance. Without her this book would not have been created. Special thanks also go to Betty Gibbs, who tirelessly edited and patiently consulted with us throughout the writing process.

Thanks to Claudia Bordeleau for the design and illustrations, which are sure to pique students' interest, and to Wendy Johnson for the meticulously created maps that greatly enhance the text.

Thanks also to Hanna Mizuno and Faye Zeidman of the Dufferin-Clark branch of the York Region Public Library, for their invaluable help during the research phase of the book.

We would both like to thank our families for their understanding when time was at a premium and for their patience, support and encouragement throughout.

## Project Team

*Project Managers:* Karen Iversen, Betty Gibbs
*Editors:* Betty Gibbs, Karen Iversen, Shauna Babiuk
*Cover and text design:*
Obsidian Multimedia Corporation, Claudia Bordeleau
*Photo research:* David Strand, assisted by Laraine Coates
*Production:* Tracy Menzies, Jeff Miles
*Maps and illustrations:*
Johnson Cartographics Inc., Wendy Johnson
Obsidian Multimedia Corporation, Claudia Bordeleau
Some images from Corel, Photospin, Eyewire and Photodisc.
*Photographer:* New Visions Photography, Brad Callihoo
*Photo Shoot Coordinator:* Roberta Wildgoose

## Manufacturers

Screaming Colour Inc., Quality Color Press

## Photographic Models

| | | | |
|---|---|---|---|
| *Francis* | Eddie Chartrand | *Mrs. Patel* | Shellina Pirmohamed |
| *Luke* | Ethan Flett | *Lincoln* | Gouled Omar |
| *Annie* | Allison Iriye | *Madeleine* | Kay Rollans |
| *Lorie* | Jillian Oliver | *Robert* | Brett Zon |

## Picture Credits

Every effort has been made to identify and credit all sources. The publisher would appreciate notification of any omissions or errors so that they may be corrected.

Legend
(t) = top  (r) = right  (l) = left  (b) = bottom
B&M = Barrett & MacKay Photography Inc.
GNP = Grasslands National Park
SLSMC = St. Lawrence Seaway Management Corporation
TM = Tessa Macintosh
MMG = Murray M. Gillespie
DK/G = Dan Koegler/Geovisuals

All images are copyright© of their respective copyright holders, as listed below. Reproduced with permission.

If not listed below, photos are by DigitalVision (**cover**), Digital Stock (**25** ml/**36** l/**125** r), Corbis (**128** tr, tl/**130** ml) or Corel (all others).
Photos of Francis, Luke, Annie, Lorie, Mrs. Singh, Lincoln, Madeleine, Robert, the bread basket on **36**, the amythest on **58** and the fruit basket on **76** taken by New Visions Photography, Brad Callihoo.
Provincial coats of arms, flags, flowers and birds reproduced in Chapter 9 are from the Department of Canadian Heritage.

**4** (both) DK/G **6** © WorldSat International -- www.worldsat.ca -- 2001. All rights reserved. **7** (all but 3, 5, 6) DK/G (3) Kevin Morris Photography (5) MMG **17** (t, m) DK/G **18** (all) Gary Fiegehen **19** Gary Fiegehen **20** (t) Emily Carr, *Above the Trees*, c. 1935-1939, oil on paper, Vancouver Art Gallery, Emily Carr Trust VAG 42.3.83 (Photo: Trevor Mills) (b) Box [AA2170 A-B]; *Raven as a Boy Taking Salmon from the Beaver's Lake*, by Steven R. Collison, late twentieth century; carved argillite; L:16.0xW:10.2 cm **21** (t, mr, b) Gary Fiegehen (ml) Jared Hobbs **24** (tr) Western Canada Wilderness Committee File Photo/L. Allen **25** (mr) Courtesy Highland Valley Copper **26** (t) Jared Hobbs (m) Gary Fiegehen (b) DK/G **29** (t) TM (m) www.grandmaison.mb.ca (b) GNP/Brad Muir **30** (l) GNP (r) www.grandmaison.mb.ca **32, 33** Taken from *A Prairie Alphabet*, illustrations copyright © 1992 by Yvette Moore, published by Tundra Books. **34** (tr) GNP (ml, br) B&M **35** (t) Courtesy Potash Corporation of Saskatchewan, Inc. (m) Courtesy Petro-Canada **36** (ml) www.grandmaison.mb.ca **39** (t, ml, b) TM (mr) Kevin Morris Photography **40** (all) TM **41** (t) J. Kobalenko/Firstlight.ca (mr) B&M (b) TM **43** (t) Tessa Macintosh (m) "Walrus Hunt," 1987 by Jimmy "Smith" Arnamissak, reproduced with permission of La Fédération des Coopératives du Nouveau-Québec/Tookalook Native Arts **45** (t) TM (ml) Courtesy Cominco Ltd. (b) Les Photographes KEDL Ltée **47** (t) Courtesy Petro-Canada (mr) Kevin Morris Photography (ml) Jeanette Doucet **48** (t) TM (ml) Kevin Morris Photography (mr) Wolfgang Weber/GNWT **51** (t) Lawren Harris, *First Snow, North Shore of Lake Superior*, 1923, oil on canvas, Vancouver Art Gallery, Founders Fund VAG 50.4 (Photo: Trevor Mills). Reproduced with permission of Mrs. Margaret Knox. (b) Parks Canada/W. Wyett **53** (tl, tr) TM (ml) Parks Canada (mr) www.grandmaison.mb.ca **56** (t) Courtesy Manitoba Hydro (ml) B&M (bl) Grant Black/Firstlight.ca (br) Brian Milne/Firstlight.ca **57** (all) Photos by Jack Humphrey of JaxGrafix. **59** (t, ml, mr) City of Greater Sudbury, Economic Development and Planning Services (b) City of Greater Sudbury and Don Johnston **60** (tl, ml) A Giardini, Toronto Catholic District School Board (bl) City of Greater Sudbury, Economic Development and Planning Services (all r) www.grandmaison.mb.ca **63** (all) MMG **64** (tl, m) www.grandmaison.mb.ca (tr, b) MMG **65** (all) MMG **66** (t) MMG (ml) Courtesy Manitoba Hydro (mr, b) www.grandmaison.mb.ca **67** (all) Kara Fry and staff of St. Ann's School, Fort Albany. **68** (t) www.grandmaison.mb.ca (ml, b) Courtesy Manitoba Hydro (mr) www.grandmaison.mb.ca **71** (m) B&M (b) Parks Canada **73** (t) SLSMC/Thies Bogner (b) SLSMC **74** (t) SLSMC/Clayton Mockler **75** (all but tr) Parks Canada **76** (tr, m) B&M **77** (t) "The Road Less Travelled" freeform embroidered quilt by Bridget O'Flaherty, Perth, Ontario. (b) "Envelopes" contemporary quilt by Bridget O'Flaherty, Perth, Ontario. **78** (all but bl) Waterfront Regeneration Trust **81** (m) Parks Canada/Gary Briand/1010-02 **82** (all) B&M **83** (t) B&M (b) Photo by Boily **84** (all) B&M **85** (l) CP Picture Archive (J.H. Strjoh) (r) B&M **86** (all) B&M **88** (all) B&M **92** (ml) B&M **97** (b) B&M **98** (b) Gerald Holdsworth **100** (b) Kevin Morris Photography **101** (b) www.grandmaison.mb.ca **103** (b) B&C Alexander/Firstlight.ca **105** (t) www.grandmaison.mb.ca **110** (b) B&M **111** (b) B&M **115** (t) Office of the Lieutenant Governor of Ontario (b) CP Picture Archive (Dave Buston) **116** (t) Government of Nunavut (b) Legislative Assembly of Ontario **120** (tl) www.grandmaison.mb.ca (tr) Department of National Defense (bl) CP Picture Archive (J.H. Strjoh) **122** (all but mr) B&M (mr) Courtesy Economic Development Edmonton **125** (tl) B&M (tr) Courtesy Toyota Motor Manufacturing Canada **128** (ml) ©2001 NBA Entertainment. Photo by Ron Turenne (mr) Courtesy Mercury Records (b) B&M **129** (tl) Les Photographes KEDL Ltée (tr) Courtesy National Ballet School (b) CP Picture Archive (Ryan Remiorz) **130** (mr) Photo from NASA **131** (tr) Kevin Morris Photography (bl) ©RCMP-GRC (2001) (br) Courtesy Westcoast Energy Inc. **132** (tr) Canadian National Exhibition 2001 (m) Department of National Defense

## Text Acknowledgments

**20** "And My Heart Soars," by Chief Dan George. Copyright © 1974, 1989 Hancock House Publishers Ltd., 19313 Zero Avenue, Surrey, BC.
**42** "The Gift of the Whale," from *Native American Animal Stories*, by Joseph Bruchac. Copyright © 1992 Fulcrum Publishing Inc., Golden, Colorado, USA. Reproduced with permission. All rights reserved.
**77** "Patterns" by B. Gibbs.
**87** "The Newfoundland Cod," from *Don't Eat Spiders*. Copyright © 1985 by Robert Heidbreder. Reproduced by permission of Stoddart Publishing Company Ltd., Toronto.

## To the Student

Canada is a large and varied country. Canadians are fortunate to have many different environments in which to live. In different places the land takes different forms. For example, some types of landforms are high mountains, wide flat plains and rolling hills.

The surfaces of the landforms are clothed with many different types of plants. Thick forests, waving fields of grasses, rich farmlands and bare fields of ice describe just a few different places in Canada.

The weather varies a great deal in different places. Summer weather may be hot and sweltering. The southern, more humid areas of Canada are often like that. It may be cool and sunny, as northern communities often are. Near an ocean, winter may be mild, cool and wet. In other places, winter may be icy cold, with a whipping wind.

Canadians live in 13 provinces and territories that are all part of the same country. The provinces and territories of Canada are connected to each other in many ways. Some examples are roads and railroads, telephone lines and television networks. Canadians buy and sell products and provide services to other people. These are also connections.

We invite you to look at the different sides of Canada with seven student hosts and their leader, Mrs. Patel. They will help you learn how places in Canada are both similar and different. The notes, interviews, photographs, charts and diagrams will help you understand the different environments in Canada and the people who live in them. Throughout the book, the student hosts will also introduce you to environmental issues that affect the future of our country.

Social Studies helps us learn about different places and different ways that people live. We hope that your knowledge and appreciation of Canada will grow from working with this book.

### The Canada Project

Your class will be working on a project about Canada's provinces and territories. You will learn more about the project at the end of Chapter 1.

# Contents

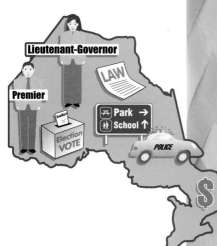

# Chapter 1
# Let's Look at Canada

Hello, everybody! It's wonderful to have you here. Welcome to the Chateau Laurier. It's a hotel in Ottawa, Ontario, the capital of Canada!

Seven students have been invited here to a conference to share information with you about the parts of Canada they come from. Together we are going to build a picture of our country.

Before we do anything else, we will introduce ourselves and show you on this map where we come from. I am Mrs. Sulema Patel, and I am from Ottawa. I will be leading you during this conference.

## Focus on Learning

In this chapter, you will learn about
- the words to describe the physical regions of Canada
- how to make comparisons
- the parts of a map
- how to gather information from maps
- how to make a map
- the boundaries of the provinces and territories of Canada

## Vocabulary

| | | |
|---|---|---|
| environment | cross-section | compass rose |
| region | physical | cardinal |
| political region | features | directions |
| boundary | landforms | intermediate |
| physical region | climate | directions |
| map | vegetation | legend |
| relief map | natural | scale |
| elevation | resource | |

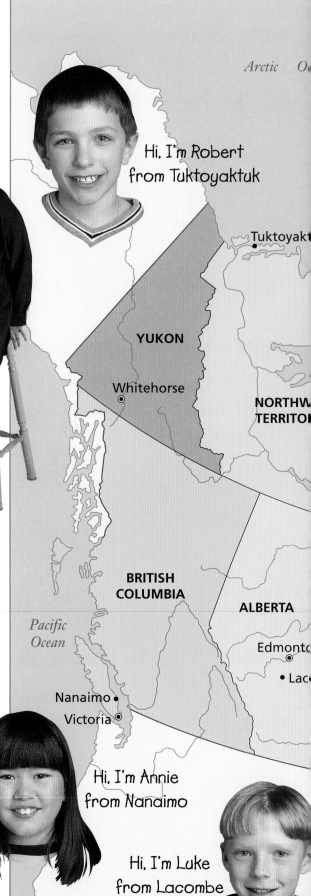

Hi, I'm Robert from Tuktoyaktuk

Hi, I'm Annie from Nanaimo

Hi, I'm Luke from Lacombe

**Political Map of Canada**

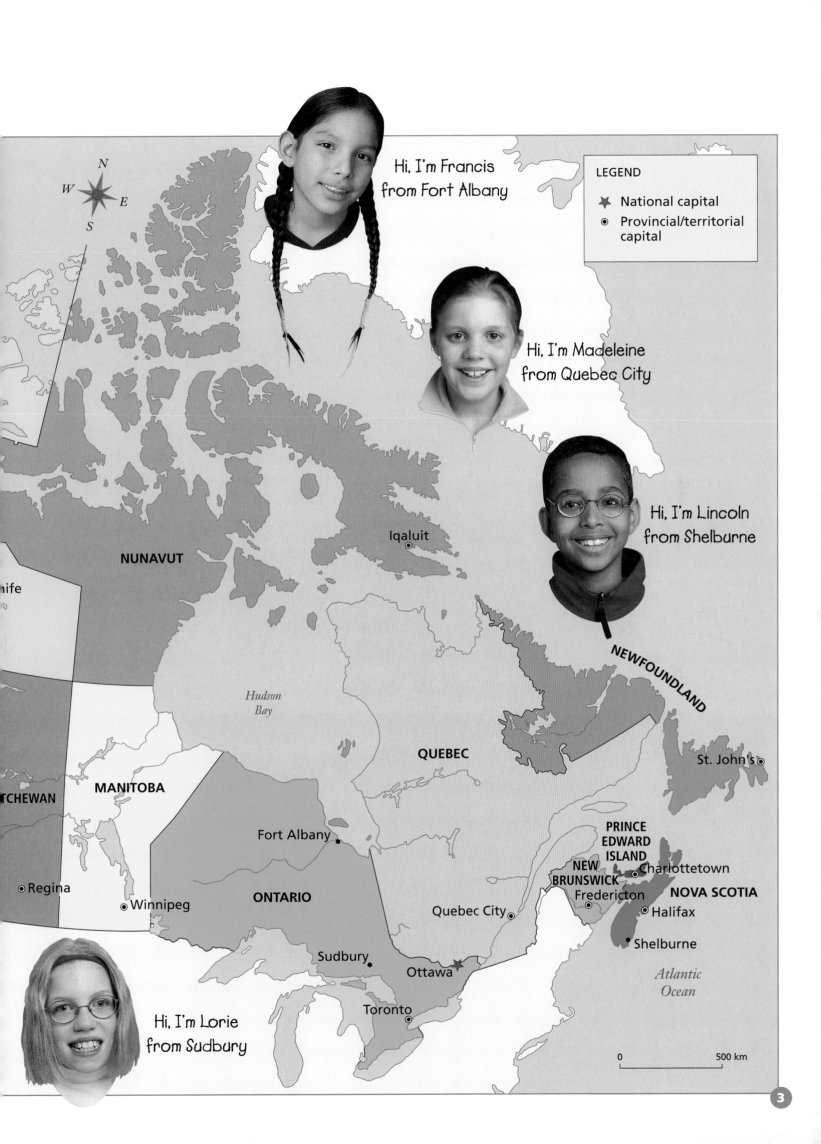

Hi, I'm Francis from Fort Albany

Hi, I'm Madeleine from Quebec City

Hi, I'm Lincoln from Shelburne

Hi, I'm Lorie from Sudbury

N
W · E
S

NUNAVUT

Iqaluit

NEWFOUNDLAND

Hudson Bay

QUEBEC

St. John's

ife

MANITOBA

TCHEWAN

Fort Albany

PRINCE EDWARD ISLAND

NEW BRUNSWICK

Charlottetown

⊙ Regina

⊙ Winnipeg

ONTARIO

NOVA SCOTIA

Fredericton

Quebec City

Halifax

Sudbury

Shelburne

Ottawa

Atlantic Ocean

Toronto

0 ——————— 500 km

3

# Studying Our Environment

I am a geographer. I study the environment that surrounds us. I study how it affects us and how we also affect the environment. For example, the weather in the place where I live affects the kind of house I will build.

Choices that we make can affect our environment and other people. For example, you may want to farm the land on which you live. But what if there is not enough rain or a source of water to grow strong, healthy crops? You might dig a canal and change the way a stream flows. This would affect the environment and other people.

 Skills & Tools

We use special tools and skills in Social Studies to learn about people, the places they live and their ways of life. We use maps, photographs, and images to look at countries and landforms. We study graphs, charts and diagrams to learn about people and their environments (their surroundings).

This landscape has been formed by natural forces and changed very little by people.

The straight roads, the pattern made by cutting grain fields and the farm buildings show that this environment has been changed by people.

# Regions of Canada

Canada is the second largest country in the world. The land area is 9 093 507 square kilometres. There are thousands of lakes and thousands of kilometres of rivers.

It is difficult to look at a country as large as Canada without breaking it up into smaller parts. Regions are areas that are similar throughout. They are different from the places around them. There are many types of regions. In this book we will look at political regions and physical regions.

## Two Types of Regions

A political region is an area with agreed-upon boundaries and its own government. A boundary is the outline of an area. It shows where the area begins and ends. We call the political regions of Canada "provinces" and "territories."

A physical region is a part of the Earth where the environment is similar throughout and different from the regions beside it.

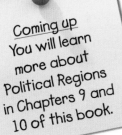

Coming up
You will learn more about Political Regions in Chapters 9 and 10 of this book.

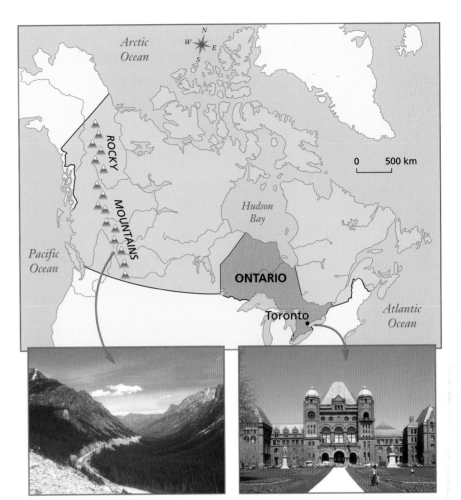

The Rocky Mountains are in a physical region. Mountains are a characteristic of the region.

Ontario is a political region. This is the Legislative Assembly in Toronto, where the Ontario government meets.

## Do ◆ Discuss ◆ Discover

1. a) Working in pairs, create a list of all of the provinces and territories of Canada that you know. Write them in your notebook.
   b) How many provinces are there?
   c) How many territories are there?
   d) What is the total?

2. Use the map inside the front cover of this textbook to check your answers. Fill in any that you have missed.

3. Label the provinces and territories on an outline map of Canada. Locate and label the places where the seven children come from. (Check pages 2 and 3 for these.)

# Reading a Satellite Image

Satellites provide us with images of the surface of the Earth. They are taken from many hundreds of kilometres in space. This is an image of Canada taken from a satellite. The colours are not true to life. The colours represent information that the satellite records about the Earth. Look at the image carefully. Can you find some places in Canada that you can see from a satellite?

Mountains, large bodies of water, ice, land and the shapes of the ocean floor are recorded in this satellite image.

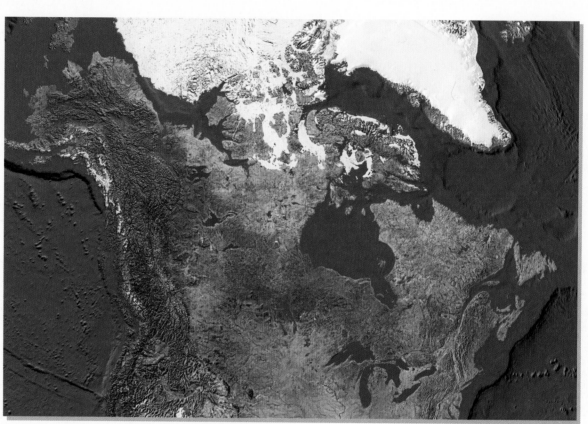

**Satellite Image of Canada**

## Do ◆ Discuss ◆ Discover

1. With a partner, try to find these places on the satellite image. (You may need to use an atlas to be sure.)

   a) Pacific Ocean
   b) Atlantic Ocean
   c) Rocky Mountains
   d) Great Lakes

   e) areas of permanent ice
   f) Newfoundland
   g) Hudson Bay
   h) St. Lawrence Seaway

2. Answer these questions in your notebook and share your answers with one other student.

   a) What do you think the green colour represents?

   b) What do you think the other colours represent?

   c) Describe two facts about Canada using information from this image.

# A Relief Map of Canada

A **map** is a drawing that shows the surface of the Earth from above. Different maps show different information about the surface of the Earth.

The map on this page is a **relief map**. A relief map shows you what land is flat and what is hilly or mountainous. All places that are certain heights above sea level are coloured the same. This shows what the surface of the land looks like. The legend of the map shows you what **elevations** are represented by each colour. Elevation is the height above sea level of a place.

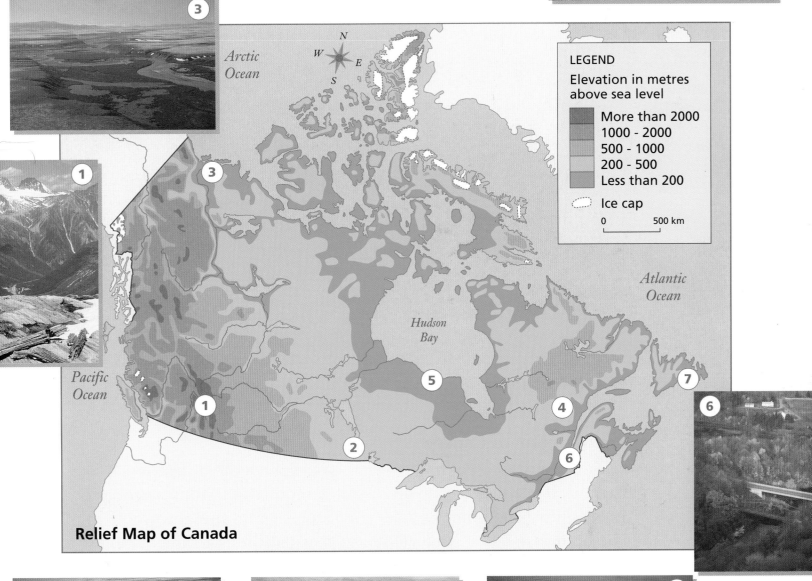

**LEGEND**

Elevation in metres above sea level

More than 2000
1000 - 2000
500 - 1000
200 - 500
Less than 200

Ice cap

0        500 km

Arctic Ocean

Pacific Ocean

Hudson Bay

Atlantic Ocean

**Relief Map of Canada**

# Physical Regions of Canada

A physical region is a part of the Earth where the environment is similar throughout and different from the regions around it.

For example, the Canadian Shield physical region can be described as a large area of rocky hills and lakes. The Interior Plains region is a large area of nearly level ground with long rivers running through it.

Some regions have high elevation and others are close to sea level.

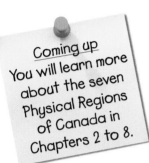

Coming up
You will learn more about the seven Physical Regions of Canada in Chapters 2 to 8.

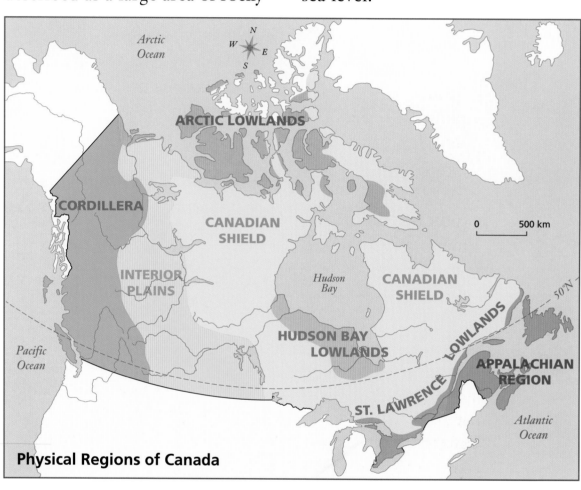

**Physical Regions of Canada**

## Cross-section of Canada

This is a cross-section diagram. It is a slice of Canada showing its shape from the side. The bottom line is at sea level. The heights of the mountains and hills are exaggerated. This way you can see the differences in the elevations of regions more easily. The diagram shows a profile of Canada along the line of dashes marked on the Physical Regions map above.

| Cordillera | Interior Plains | Canadian Shield | Appalachian |

0        500 km

# Describing Physical Regions

A physical region has similar physical features, climate, vegetation, animal life and natural resources throughout it.

**Physical features** are the landforms and bodies of water in a place.

The highest **landforms** are mountains. A mountain range is a line of mountains. Valleys are low areas between mountains or hills.

Landforms that are high but flat are called plateaus. Plateaus are often found between two mountain ranges.

Hills are rounded landforms that are smaller than mountains. Plains are low flat areas. In western Canada, the large area of plains is also called the prairies.

Bodies of water include oceans, lakes and rivers. There are many other names for special types of water bodies. For example, a sea is a body of salt water, smaller than an ocean, that is partly enclosed by land.

**Climate** is the average pattern of weather over many years. Temperature and precipitation (rain, snow, sleet) are both parts of climate.

**Vegetation** is all of the plants that naturally grow in a place. The climate of a place affects the plants that grow there. If there are few warm days, little will grow. If there is lots of rain and warm weather, plants will grow large. If it is hot and dry, like a desert, only special desert plants will grow.

The **animal life** of a region includes animals, birds, fish and other living creatures. A region beside an ocean will have both land animals and marine (water) animals.

**Natural resources** are materials taken from nature. We use them to make our lives easier and more enjoyable. Some natural resources are forests, water, minerals, soil and fish.

# Reading a Map

A map is a drawing that represents the Earth's surface seen from above. A **cartographer** is a person whose occupation is making maps. When you make a map, there are certain parts that you must remember to add. They give information to the person who is reading the map.

**Boundaries** outline places. Different types of boundaries use different kinds of lines.

**Lines** on a map have many uses. These include boundaries, rivers and transportation routes.

**Labels** name physical features and places. Physical features include names of rivers, oceans, deserts, mountains and other parts of the environment. Places include names of countries, provinces, cities and towns.

**Physical Regions of Canada**

The **title** tells what information is included in the map.

Lines of **latitude** are parallel lines that run East–West. Lines of **longitude** run North–South, reaching from the North Pole to the South Pole. Lines of latitude and longitude form a **grid** that helps us to locate places on the map.

A **compass rose** shows the directions on a map. A very simple compass rose just shows where North is. All maps should show North at the top of the page. Some compass roses include both the **cardinal directions** and the **intermediate directions**. The cardinal directions are North, South, East and West. The intermediate directions are between them; for example, North-West.

The **legend** of a map explains the symbols, colours and lines used on the map.

The **scale** of a map compares a distance measured on the map with a distance on the surface of the Earth.

**Colours** identify areas that have something in common.

LEGEND

▲ Mountains
⋮⋮⋮ Wetlands
⌒ Permanent ice cap

0        500 km

20°W
20°W
60°N
30°W
40°W
30°W
40°N
60°W
70°W
70°N

ADIAN IELD

LOWLANDS

APPALACHIAN REGION

VRENCE

Lawrence River

St.

Lake Ontario

Atlantic Ocean

## Do ◆ Discuss ◆ Discover

1. What is the title of the map on these pages? What information does the title give us? What information would a map with the title "Vegetation Regions of Canada" include?
2. Identify three different labels shown on the map.
3. What colour are the rivers and bodies of water?
4. Identify an example of a boundary on this map.
5. Look for the compass rose on this map. One intermediate direction is North-West. What do you think the others are?
6. Describe three ways that lines are used on this map.
7. What is the symbol used to represent mountains? What other symbols are shown in the legend of this map?

# Comparison

An **organizer** is a chart that helps us show how information about something is related. Two types of organizers are described below.

A **comparison chart** is an organizer used to compare two or more things. It shows the ways they are the same and different. To compare two things, we first decide what characteristics of the things are important to us. These are the comparison **criteria**.

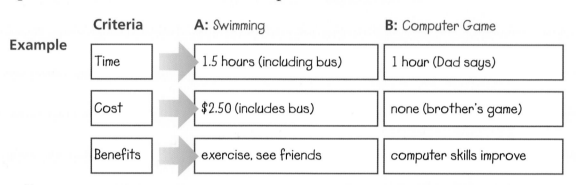

| | Criteria | A: Swimming | B: Computer Game |
|---|---|---|---|
| **Example** | Time | 1.5 hours (including bus) | 1 hour (Dad says) |
| | Cost | $2.50 (includes bus) | none (brother's game) |
| | Benefits | exercise, see friends | computer skills improve |

List the criteria on your organizer. Carefully look at the two things you are comparing. Write down what you find out beside the appropriate criteria.

A **Venn diagram** is another way of comparing things. It is made up of two overlapping circles. In the middle space, you write the characteristics shared by both things that you are comparing. These are ways the two things are the same. In the outside parts of the circles, you write the characteristics that are different.

**Example**

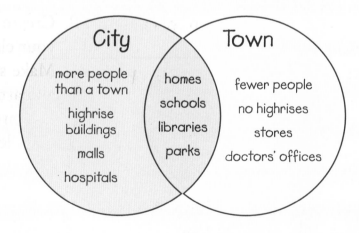

City
more people than a town
highrise buildings
malls
hospitals

homes
schools
libraries
parks

Town
fewer people
no highrises
stores
doctors' offices

## Do ◆ Discuss ◆ Discover

With a partner, do either number 1 or 2.

1. Draw a blank comparison chart organizer in your notes. Choose three criteria for comparing the satellite image on page 6 and the relief map of Canada on page 7. Complete the comparison.

2. Use a Venn diagram to compare the relief map on page 7 with the political map on pages 2 and 3.

# Chapter 1

## Understanding Concepts

1.  a) Begin a vocabulary section in your notebook. Create a title page and/or a divider in your binder to mark it. Add to this section throughout your study.

    b) In pairs, look at the vocabulary presented on page 2. Use "map" and "region" as category words. Try to list other words under the two category words.

2.  Look at the comparison chart or Venn diagram you created on page 12. In your notebook, write two statements about what you discovered using the organizer.

3.  In two or three sentences in your notebook, explain the difference between physical and political regions.

## Developing Inquiry/Research and Communication Skills

4.  Find examples of three different types of maps in books, magazines and newspapers. Examine the three maps to see if they have included the parts needed on all maps. Share your examples with a partner.

## Developing Map/Globe Skills

5.  Create a checklist of the parts of a map to put in your notebook. You can use this checklist as a reminder every time you make a map on your own.

6.  Identify, colour and label the different physical regions of Canada on an outline map of Canada. Put this map in your notebook.

7.  Create a word collage on an outline map of Canada. Think of words that describe what you have learned about Canada in this chapter, and what you already knew. Write those words all over the map. Use colour and interesting lettering. Share your collage with another student.

## Applying Concepts and Skills in Various Contexts

8.  Create a map of your classroom. Make sure that all parts of a map are included.

## Internet Connection

9.  Try the Canada Quiz on www.statcan.ca

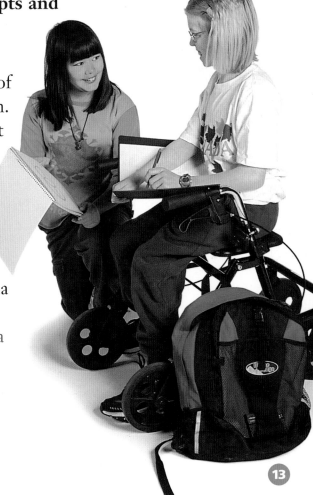

# Doing a Research Project

A major research project may be done in stages over many weeks. Often you will work on it with a group or partner.

To do research you must begin with a topic. Then you locate and gather information about it, organize it and present your information.

The following steps will help you to properly complete a research project.

## TOPIC

### Step One – Prepare for Research

1. Talk to your teacher to ensure that you understand exactly what you must do.

### Step Two – Gather Information from Various Sources

1. Plan how your project will be organized.

2. Decide how and where to gather information. Try the library, magazines, Internet sites and people with knowledge.

3. Record the information, keeping track of where you found it.

### Step Three – Organize Your Information

1. Reread the information that you have gathered.

2. Choose the information that applies best to your topic.

3. Use charts or diagrams to help you organize your thinking.

4. Write out the information in an organized way.

### Step Four – Present Your Information

1. Create materials that give information about your topic. They may be in writing, pictures, organizers, diagrams, models, objects, audio tape or videotape.

2. Decide how you will present your materials.

3. Present your information to the rest of the class.

4. Get feedback from the class. Reflect on your project and discuss how it could have been improved.

# The Canada Project

You are learning about the physical regions of Canada, the provinces and territories, and connections between parts of our country. You will be gathering, organizing and creating materials for a class project as you learn.

There are three main parts to the project. You will work with a small group on most of it. At the end of each chapter there is a reminder of work to do or collect for your final project.

## The Scrapbook

In a scrapbook, you should include the following items. You may come up with some ideas of your own as well!

- notes on the province or territory assigned to your group
- a map of the province or territory with important features and places labelled
- symbols of the province or territory's resources and products
- poems or stories you find, or your own poems or stories about your province/territory

- pictures or postcards you find, or your own pictures
- a flow chart of connections between your province or territory and other provinces and territories
- fact cards (like baseball cards) featuring key cities in your province or territory

## The Shoe Box

You will collect objects, maps, fact sheets and symbols to put in your group's shoe box. As part of the final presentation, each group will present the items in their boxes to the rest of the class. Your scrapbook information will help you with your presentation.

## The Relief Model

Your class will create together a large relief model of Canada. It will show the provinces and territories and the connections between them. Your teacher will help you make the pattern for your part so the model will all fit together. Each group will create a three-dimensional relief model of their province or territory. You will help put the relief model together as a class.

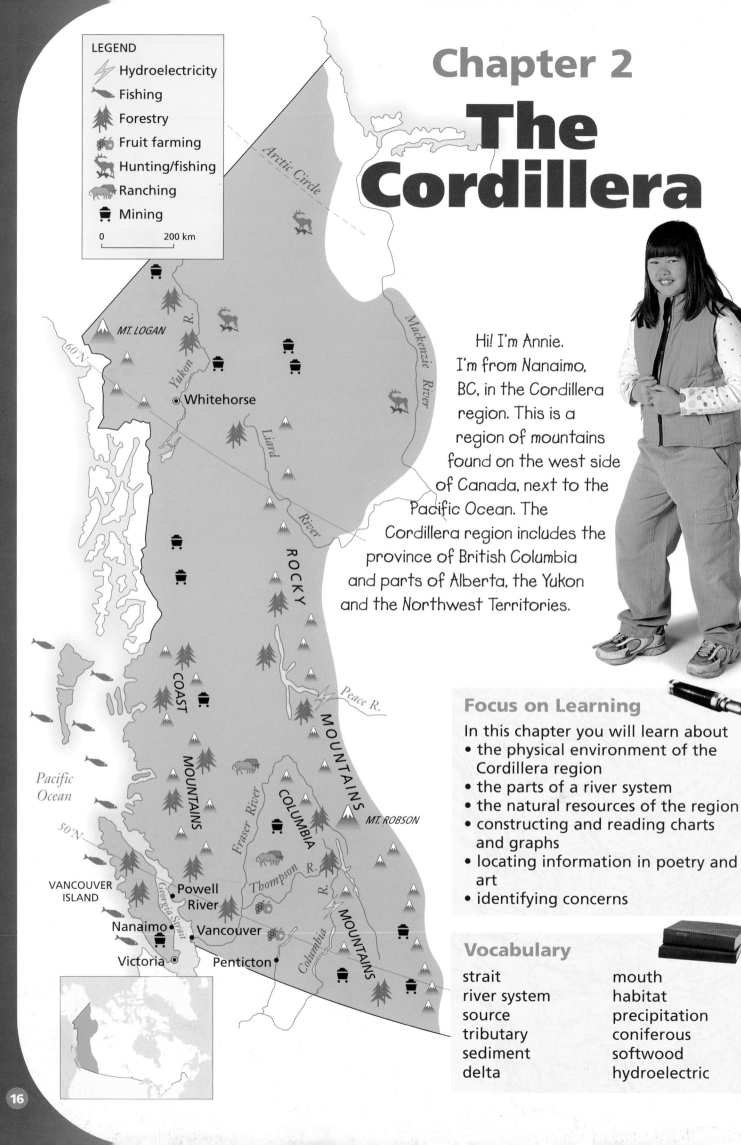

# The Cordillera

**LEGEND**
- ⚡ Hydroelectricity
- 🐟 Fishing
- 🌲 Forestry
- Fruit farming
- Hunting/fishing
- Ranching
- Mining

0          200 km

MT. LOGAN

Yukon R.

60°N

Arctic Circle

Mackenzie River

⊙ Whitehorse

Liard River

ROCKY

COAST MOUNTAINS

Pacific Ocean

50°N

VANCOUVER ISLAND

Fraser River

COLUMBIA

MT. ROBSON

MOUNTAINS

Thompson R.

Peace R.

Columbia R.

MOUNTAINS

Powell River

Nanaimo ●  Georgia Strait

Vancouver ●

Victoria ⊙

Penticton ●

Hi! I'm Annie. I'm from Nanaimo, BC, in the Cordillera region. This is a region of mountains found on the west side of Canada, next to the Pacific Ocean. The Cordillera region includes the province of British Columbia and parts of Alberta, the Yukon and the Northwest Territories.

## Focus on Learning

In this chapter you will learn about
- the physical environment of the Cordillera region
- the parts of a river system
- the natural resources of the region
- constructing and reading charts and graphs
- locating information in poetry and art
- identifying concerns

## Vocabulary

| | |
|---|---|
| strait | mouth |
| river system | habitat |
| source | precipitation |
| tributary | coniferous |
| sediment | softwood |
| delta | hydroelectric |

# Physical Features

Millions of years ago, huge folds of rock pushed up to form mountain ranges called the Cordillera. The folds bent and crushed against each other.

The Cordillera region today has many different landforms. There are mountains, hills, plateaus and valleys. Most of the region is high above sea level. There are lakes of all sizes and major river systems. The Pacific Ocean lies along the western coast.

The interior plateau lies between the Columbia Mountains and the Coast Mountains. Several large rivers flow across this high country. Then they flow through the Coast Mountains to the ocean.

Mount Robson is the highest peak in the Rocky Mountains. It is 3954 metres high.

A narrow passage of water between two larger bodies of water is a strait.

The interior plateau is fairly flat or hilly.

## Do ◆ Discuss ◆ Discover

Look at the map of the Cordillera Region on the previous page to answer these questions in your notebook.

1. Which range of mountains is found along the coastline?
2. Which range of mountains is the farthest away from the coast?
3. What body of water is found between Vancouver Island and the mainland?
4. Name two rivers shown on the map.

The Cordillera region has several mountain ranges. The highest mountains in Canada are found there.

# A River System

## The Fraser River

The Fraser River system is the largest in the Cordillera region.

The Fraser River has its source in a high area in the Rocky Mountains near Jasper National Park. It flows across the interior plateau and throughout the Coast Mountains. It ends at sea level in the Pacific Ocean.

The Fraser River is a swift-flowing river. There are waterfalls and rapids in places where it flows downhill abruptly.

Water from the surrounding land areas drains into the river and the amount of water increases. More water enters the river from other streams. The swift water carries particles of rock and soil called **sediment**.

When the river reaches flatter land, it flows more slowly. Sediment carried by the river drops to the riverbed. Over thousands of years, valleys have partly filled up and formed flat land.

The Fraser River flows down through mountain valleys to its mouth at the Pacific Ocean.

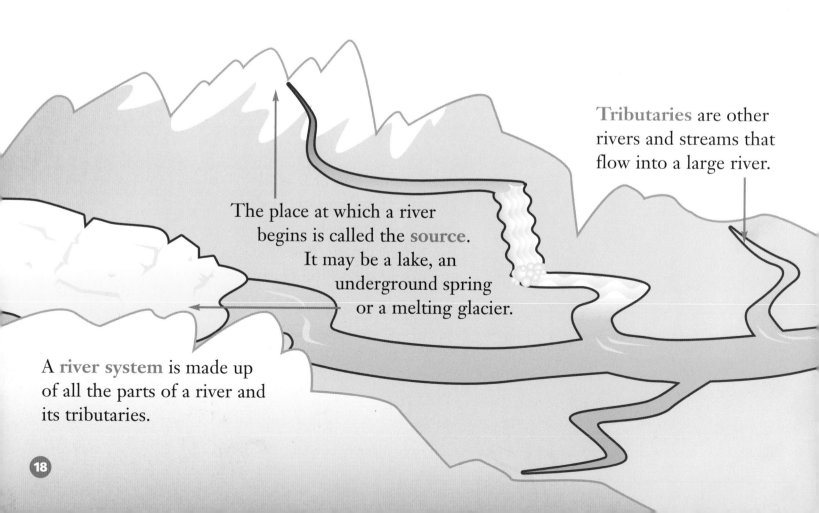

**Tributaries** are other rivers and streams that flow into a large river.

The place at which a river begins is called the **source**. It may be a lake, an underground spring or a melting glacier.

A **river system** is made up of all the parts of a river and its tributaries.

The Stein River is a tributary flowing into the Fraser River.

The Fraser River valley is widest at the mouth of the river. A large delta has formed there from sediment carried by the river. The soil of the delta is excellent farmland for produce and dairy farms.

The city of Vancouver and many smaller communities have been built in this area.

The Fraser River is the **habitat** of salmon and other fish. It provides fresh water for growing crops and drinking water. The river is also used for recreation. Some parts of it can be used for travel and transportation.

## Do ◆ Discuss ◆ Discover

1. With a partner, discuss the parts of a river system. In your notebook, list and describe each of the main parts.
2. Sketch or trace the river system diagram onto a piece of blank paper. Label all the parts. Put it in your notebook.

## Hands On!

Work with a group to create a model of the river system in the diagram on these two pages.

You will need
- a 30 x 24 cm piece of cardboard or wood
- plasticene in blue, green, brown
- a heavy plastic placemat to work on

1. Begin creating a model by using the blue plasticene to make the river and tributaries. Use the illustration on the two pages to guide you. Remember, some parts of the river are higher above sea level than others. The water will flow faster in some places. (How could you show that the water is flowing faster?)
2. When you have finished creating the river system on the board, fill in the surrounding land.
3. Once your model is finished, use small pieces of paper to label the important parts of the river system: source, tributaries, delta, mouth.

A **delta** is an area of flat land at the mouth of the river. Several branches of the river may flow through it to the ocean.

The **mouth** of a river is the place it empties into an ocean.

## Cordillera Arts

### And My Heart Soars

The beauty of the trees,
The softness of the air,
The fragrance of the grass,
Speaks to me.

The summit of the mountain,
The thunder of the sky,
The rhythm of the sea,
Speaks to me.

The faintness of the stars,
The freshness of the morning,
The dewdrop on the flower,
Speaks to me.

The strength of fire,
The taste of salmon,
The trail of the sun,
And the life that never goes
away,

They speak to me.
And my heart soars.

– Chief Dan George

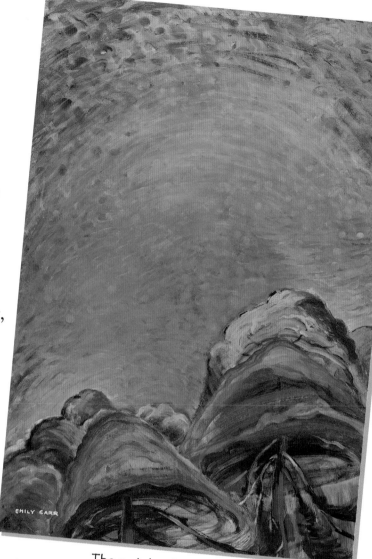

The painter Emily Carr created beautiful images of the environment of British Columbia such as this painting called Above the Trees.

This argillite stone carving called Boy Taking Salmon from Beaver's Lake was carved by Steven R. Collison.

### Do ◆ Discuss ◆ Discover

1. a) What does the poet tell you about the Cordillera in "And My Heart Soars"?

   b) Why do you think he says that everything speaks to him?

2. Describe how the work of each artist on this page represents the Cordillera.

# Climate

The climate of a place is the pattern of its weather over a long period. It includes both temperature and precipitation. Precipitation is moisture that falls as rain, snow or sleet.

The Cordillera region has many different climates. The northern Cordillera region has cold winters and warm summers. It gets about 200 to 400 mm of precipitation in a year.

The southern part of the region has warmer temperatures.

Heavy snowfalls are common in mountain forests.

The area along the coast has mild and rainy weather. Precipitation can be as high as 2000 mm a year. The ocean helps to keep places near the coast cooler in summer and warmer in winter.

Grasses and flowers grow on this sunny mountainside.

The mountains and valleys of the interior plateau get hot in summer. They can be quite cold in the winter.

The Pacific Coast is well-known for frequent rain and fog.

## Do ◆ Discuss ◆ Discover

Discuss the following questions with a partner.

1. Which places in the Cordillera region do you think get more rain—places near the coast or places in the interior? Which do you think get more snow? Why?

2. How are the environments in the photos on this page similar to, or different from, where you live?

# Reading Charts and Graphs

**Charts** and **graphs** are organized ways to display information. The title of a chart or graph tells you what information is being shown. The way a chart or graph is organized helps show how the information is related. In the example below, the information is organized by year.

Many charts are used to display numbers. Numbers are also called **statistics**. The numbers in the chart below represent square kilometres of forest harvested (cut down to be sold) in the Yukon Territory.

| Estimated Area of Harvested Forest Lands – Yukon Territory | | | | | |
|---|---|---|---|---|---|
| **Year** | **1992** | **1993** | **1994** | **1995** | **1996** |
| **Estimated square km** | 6.5 | 6.5 | 20.5 | 8.5 | 19.0 |

The same information can be displayed in more than one way. A graph is a visual way of showing information. It uses pictures or lines to represent numbers.

In a **picture graph**, each picture represents a certain amount. The legend shows how much each represents. In the example below, 2 square kilometres of harvested land are represented by one tree.

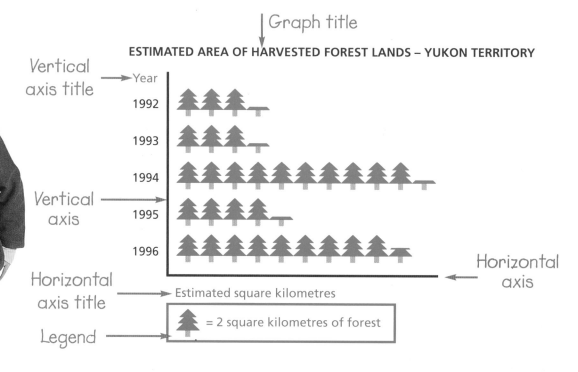

On **bar graphs**, the amounts are shown on a scale marked in units up the side. An example of a bar graph is shown on the next page. A bar graph may give information about one thing, or it may compare two or more things.

# Comparing Climates

When we compare the climates of places, we compare their average temperatures and precipitation.

## Temperature

The community of Powell River is on the coast of British Columbia. The community of Penticton is farther south in BC than Powell River. (See the map on page 16.) Use the charts on the right to study the average temperatures for these two places.

## Precipitation

Places near an ocean usually get more precipitation.

The graph on the right is a bar graph. It compares the average precipitation in winter for Powell River and Penticton. The amounts are represented by bars.

| Powell River, BC – Average Temperature in Degrees Celsius | | | | | | | | | | | |
| --- | --- | --- | --- | --- | --- | --- | --- | --- | --- | --- | --- |
| JAN | FEB | MAR | APR | MAY | JUNE | JULY | AUG | SEPT | OCT | NOV | DEC |
| 5 | 7 | 9 | 12 | 17 | 20 | 22 | 22 | 19 | 13 | 8 | 5 |

| Penticton, BC – Average Temperature in Degrees Celsius | | | | | | | | | | | |
| --- | --- | --- | --- | --- | --- | --- | --- | --- | --- | --- | --- |
| JAN | FEB | MAR | APR | MAY | JUNE | JULY | AUG | SEPT | OCT | NOV | DEC |
| 1 | 4 | 10 | 15 | 20 | 25 | 28 | 28 | 22 | 5 | 7 | 1 |

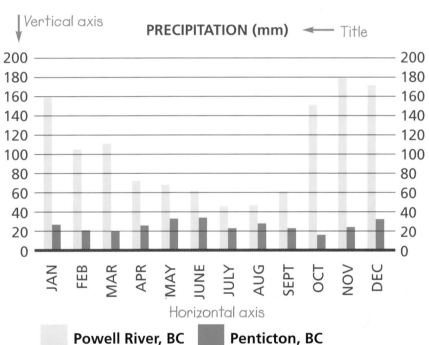

Powell River, BC    Penticton, BC

The website www.statcan.ca provides a variety of statistics about Canada.

## Do ◆ Discuss ◆ Discover

Look at the average temperature and precipitation for each season of the year for each community.

1. Which place is warmer in the summer?
2. Which place gets the most rainfall in the summer?
3. During which months is the difference in precipitation 100 millimetres or more?
4. Why do we use the word precipitation when describing climate, instead of just rain?

# Vegetation

The cool, rainy climate along the Pacific Coast is perfect for the giant trees that grow there. Most forests of the Cordillera Region are **coniferous**. Coniferous trees have needles and cones. Most coniferous trees are evergreen.

The tallest tree in Canada is a Sitka spruce 95 m tall! It is found on Vancouver Island.

The rain forest near the Pacific Coast has the largest coniferous trees in Canada.

Most plants, shrubs and trees grow larger on the coast than they do elsewhere. Flowering plants produce large, healthy blooms.

Mountain valleys of the Cordillera and some parts of the interior plateau are covered in forests. The tops of the high mountains have little vegetation. There is little soil there and fewer warm days than in the valleys.

The natural vegetation of much of the interior plateau is grassland. Many other plants grow in places where rivers and lakes provide more water.

# Animal Life

Many kinds of animals live in the land, air and water of the Cordillera region. Large parts of the region have few people in them. There is lots of food for animal life.

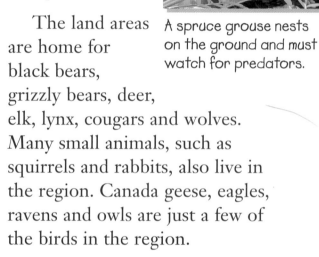

A spruce grouse nests on the ground and must watch for predators.

The land areas are home for black bears, grizzly bears, deer, elk, lynx, cougars and wolves. Many small animals, such as squirrels and rabbits, also live in the region. Canada geese, eagles, ravens and owls are just a few of the birds in the region.

Polar bears and caribou are found in the far northern parts of the Cordillera region.

The Pacific Ocean is home to many kinds of sea life. The Pacific salmon is an important food resource. Marine animals, such as whales and seals, are common along the coast of the region.

This huge sea lion seems clumsy on shore but is an excellent, graceful swimmer in the ocean.

# Natural Resources

The thickest forests and largest trees in Canada grow in the Cordillera Region. Forest resources provide the most important products in this region.

**Softwood** is timber that comes from coniferous trees. It is used to make pulp and paper products. Softwood is also used in construction. Approximately 90% of the timber produced in Canada is softwood.

Trees are made into many products, such as paper, plywood, cellophane, cardboard cartons and furniture.

*Forests are a renewable resource because they can be regrown.*

There are two giant **hydroelectric** dams on rivers in the Cordillera region. They are the Revelstoke Dam on the Columbia River and the W.A.C. Bennet Dam on the Peace River. The energy of falling water is used to create electricity.

This region has many minerals. At one time, people came from all over to search for gold in the Fraser River valley and in the Klondike River area. Gold, coal, copper, asbestos, zinc, silver, lead, sand and gravel are mined in the region. Minerals mined here are sold all over Canada and the world.

The Pacific Ocean and the rivers and lakes are the source of many kinds of fish. Salmon, halibut, herring and shellfish are important resources in the Cordillera Region.

The Okanagan Valley in the southern part of this region has good soil and a warm climate. It is famous for its orchards. Apples, pears, plums, cherries, peaches, apricots and grapes are produced there.

*31% of the copper mined in Canada comes from the Cordillera region.*

This huge vehicle is working in an open-pit copper mine, the Highland Valley mine near Kamloops, BC.

Lumber and pulp to make paper are sold to countries all over the world.

Visit www.canadiangeographic.ca to learn more about the resources in this region.

Hot summers are important for fruit crops.

# Annie's Concern

My mother is a Royal Canadian Mounted Police constable. She is often called to work with the Ministry of Natural Resources. They sometimes ask her to enforce laws controlling how and when forests are cut. I think this is an important part of what *my* mother does.

I believe our forests are important to the environment. Many animals, birds, plants and other forms of life live in them.

The forest is their habitat. If forests are cut down completely, these living things may also disappear.

I am concerned that forests are being cut down without enough planning and care for the future of our environment.

## Do ◆ Discuss ◆ Discover

1. Our forests are an important resource. What are three ways that we can care for Canada's forests?

2. The forest provides many jobs. Brainstorm what jobs are involved in the forest industry and in caring for our forests.

3. What are some ideas, images and words you might include on a poster to promote healthy forests?

# Chapter 2

## Understanding Concepts

1. Copy the following organizer into your notebook. First, put a title on the organizer. Name the physical region you are describing. Fill in every area with information that you have learned from this chapter and your notes.

| Physical Region: | |
|---|---|
| TOPICS | WHAT I LEARNED |
| Physical Features | |
| Climate | |
| Vegetation | |
| Animal Life | |
| Natural Resources | |

*Example*

2. Identify vocabulary from this chapter to add to the vocabulary section of your notebook. Draw diagrams or sketches to help you remember the words and their meanings.

## Developing Inquiry/Research and Communication Skills

3. With a partner, research jobs in the forestry industry. Follow the research model on page 14. Design a Help Wanted poster for one of the jobs you have learned about. Choose images or design ideas for getting people's attention and persuading them to apply.

## Developing Map/Globe Skills

4. Create your own picture symbols to show the natural resources found in the Cordillera region. Place them on an outline map of the region. Include a legend.

## Applying Concepts and Skills in Various Contexts

5. Imagine you are moving to the Cordillera region. Write an e-mail or a letter describing how you feel about moving there and what you are looking forward to.

## The Canada Project

1. Locate and decorate a shoebox. You will use it to hold objects, maps and other things your group collects or makes throughout your project. Make it bright, fun and interesting! Do the same thing with the cover of your group's scrapbook.

2. Begin a map of Canada. On an outline map of Canada, colour the Cordillera region. Label the provinces/territories that are in the Cordillera region. Add important information about the Cordillera region to your map. (Use the maps on page 16 and inside the front and back covers of the text to help.) You will be adding to your map as you work through Chapters 3 to 8.

3. Use an atlas to locate a river system that flows through your group's province or territory. Draw a small diagram with a brief description of it for your scrapbook.

# Chapter 3
# The Interior Plains

Hi! I'm Luke. I come from Lacombe, Alberta, in the Interior Plains region. This region stretches along the east side of the Cordillera as far north as the Arctic Ocean. It includes the western part of the Northwest Territories and large parts of Alberta, Saskatchewan and Manitoba.

## Focus on Learning

In this chapter you will learn about
- the physical environment of the Interior Plains region
- how latitude affects climate
- the natural resources important to the region
- reading and creating charts and graphs
- locating important information in pictures
- identifying concerns

## Vocabulary

glacier        herbivore
drought      carnivore
dormant     wetlands
irrigation     fertile
deciduous   erosion

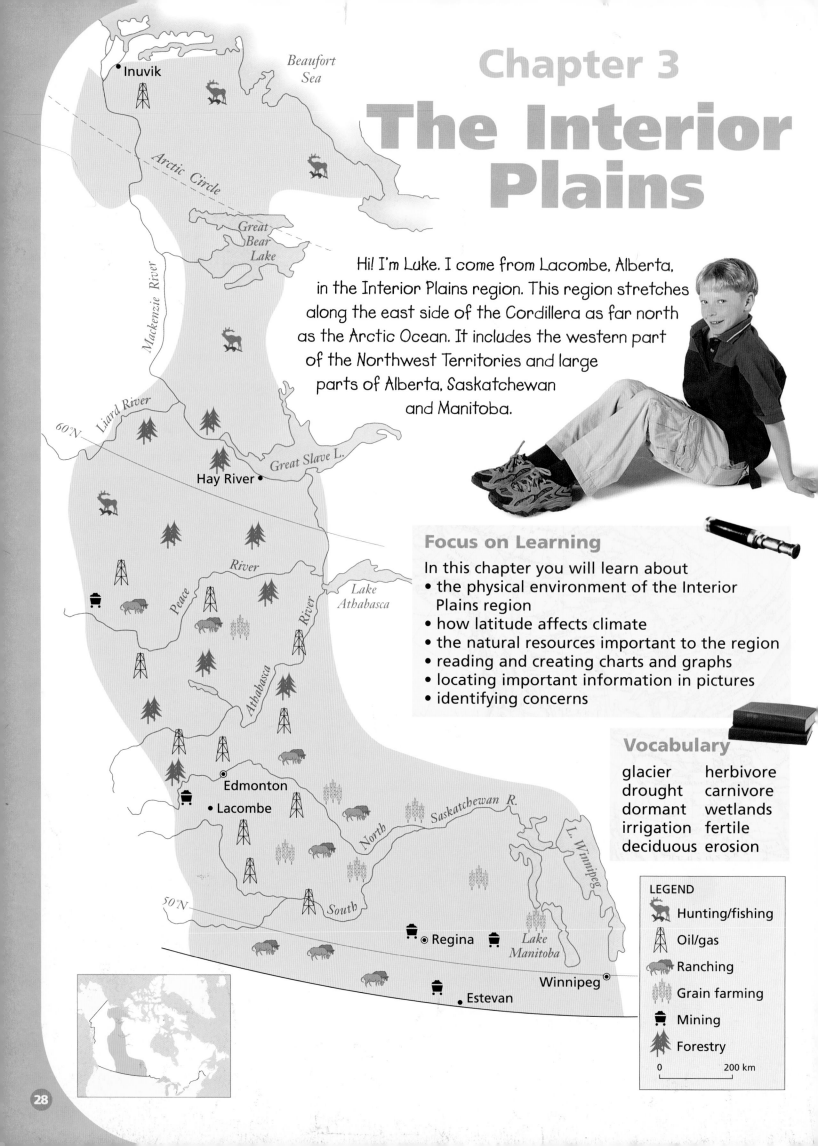

Beaufort Sea

Inuvik

Arctic Circle

Great Bear Lake

Mackenzie River

Liard River

60°N

Great Slave L.

Hay River

Peace River

Athabasca River

Lake Athabasca

Edmonton

Lacombe

North Saskatchewan R.

South Saskatchewan R.

50°N

Regina

Lake Manitoba

L. Winnipeg

Winnipeg

Estevan

### LEGEND

Hunting/fishing

Oil/gas

Ranching

Grain farming

Mining

Forestry

0        200 km

# Physical Features

The Interior Plains region is nearly flat or has rolling hills. This huge plain descends in several levels. It is highest in the foothills of the Rocky Mountains. It is almost at sea level in Manitoba and the Northwest Territories.

About 18 thousand years ago, much of Canada was covered by two huge sheets of ice. They were up to two kilometres thick in places. These **glaciers** grew very slowly as the whole Earth became cooler.

The weight of the glaciers caused the land to sink down. As the glaciers melted, huge lakes and rivers were formed. The lakes then became smaller, but many remain. Rocks, gravel, sand and silt were left behind. They formed hills and flat areas of plains.

Grasslands National Park in southwestern Saskatchewan was created to preserve the original prairie vegetation.

This region has many of the largest lakes and longest rivers in Canada. Several river systems begin in the Rocky Mountains. They flow north and east to the Arctic Ocean and Hudson Bay.

The lowest, flattest parts of the Interior Plains are the delta of the Mackenzie River and southern Manitoba.

Several large lakes are found in the northern Interior Plains.

Rivers in flat country have difficulty carrying away water because there is little downhill slope. Therefore, these flat lands often flood.

# Climate

The climate of the Interior Plains is more severe than the climate of the Cordillera. Most places have cold winters and hot summers.

The Interior Plains region has less precipitation than most other regions of Canada. Places sometimes have no rain for long periods. This is called a **drought**.

Winter in the Interior Plains can be extremely cold, with clear sunny skies.

Healthy crops need both sun and precipitation.

## Latitude

The temperature of a place is affected by where it is found on the Earth. In Canada, the farther north a place is, the colder it usually is. There are few hours of daylight in winter. The sun gives little heat. We can describe how far north a place is by saying what line of **latitude** it lies on.

Lines of latitude are imaginary parallel lines around the Earth. That means that a line of latitude joins points that are equal distances from the Equator. Lines of latitude are numbered in degrees N and degrees S, for North and South of the Equator.

Most of the southern border of Canada is formed by the latitude line 49 degrees North (49° N). There are 90 degrees between the Equator and the North Pole. All of Canada is over halfway to the North Pole. No wonder it gets cold in winter!

The symbol for degrees is °. It is used both for angles and for temperatures.

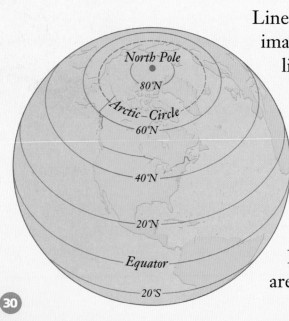

North Pole
80°N
Arctic Circle
60°N
40°N
20°N
Equator
20°S

### Do ◆ Discuss ◆ Discover

1. a) Look at an atlas to see where Canada is located compared to the Equator.

   b) What is the latitude reading for the place farthest south in Canada? What is it for the place farthest north?

# What's the Weather?

## Temperature

The temperature of places in the Interior Plains is affected by their latitude position. The chart below compares temperatures in Estevan, Saskatchewan, and Hay River, Northwest Territories. (See map on page 28.)

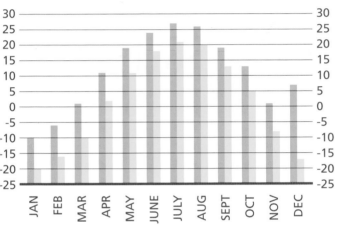

**AVERAGE TEMPERATURE IN DEGREES CELSIUS**

■ Estevan, SK　□ Hay River, NT

## Precipitation

Regina, Saskatchewan, and Powell River, BC, are both located near 50° N latitude. However, their climates are very different. In Regina the average yearly precipitation is 364 millimetres. This is an average of 30 mm each month. Look at the graph on page 23 to see the precipitation in Powell River. The illustration to the right compares the average monthly precipitation. Powell River has more precipitation because it is nearer to the ocean.

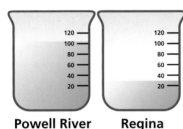

**Powell River　Regina**

## Do ◆ Discuss ◆ Discover

1. In your atlas, look up the latitude positions of Estevan and Hay River. One is much farther north. What is the difference between the two latitudes?

2. In your notebook, draw two thermometers side by side. On them, show the difference between Estevan's average temperatures in July and in January. Write one or two sentences under the thermometers describing the difference.

3. Compare the temperatures for Hay River and Estevan in April, May and June. Which place is colder? What might explain the difference?

## Hands On!

Work with a group to explore how rain happens. Ask an adult to help you with this activity.

You will need
- a large pot of water
- ice cubes
- a burner or stove top
- a small pot
- your notebook

1. Wait until the water in the large pot is boiling. Then place the ice in the smaller pot.

2. Hold the smaller pot over the large pot.

3. Watch the steam from the boiling water condense into liquid on the outside of the smaller pot.

4. When enough steam has condensed and the drops become heavy enough, they will fall into the large pot.

5. Draw diagrams in your notebook of what happened during each step of this activity. Explain your diagrams in writing.

# Reading Images

When you do research, you gather information from many sources. **Images** are one important source of information. All kinds of pictures are images. Photographs and visual arts, such as paintings, drawings and sculptures, are all images.

An artist chooses what is shown in an image. Everything that appears is there for a reason. When you "read" an image, first decide what you think its subject is. Then look at the details. Decide what the details tell you about the subject. Think about why they have been included in the image.

Look at the foreground for information. The subject of the image is often in the foreground. The most important parts of the picture are usually larger, clearer and in the middle. They catch your attention.

Look at the middle ground and the background. These show where the subject is located. They give information about the surroundings or the environment.

Images usually give you a feeling about the subject.

Illustration by Yvette Moore for A Prairie Alphabet by Jo Bannatyne-Cugnet

# Plains Arts

Illustration by Yvette Moore for A Prairie Alphabet by Jo Bannatyne-Cugnet

## Do ◆ Discuss ◆ Discover

1. What is the subject of each image on pages 32 and 33?

2. Describe the middle ground and background of each image.

3. Describe what you see in each image and how it makes you feel.

4. Draw a web for each image. Identify things in the image that represent the environment of the Interior Plains.

5. Choose either one of the images. Write a one-page story about the people and what is happening on the day this image was drawn. (If the Interior Plains is part of your province or territory, you could put this story in your scrapbook or shoebox. Otherwise put it in your notebook.)

# Vegetation

The natural vegetation of most of the southern Interior Plains is grasses. When there is drought, the grasses go brown and **dormant**. That means they wait until there is rain before putting up new green shoots. **Irrigation** is used to bring water to crops in some dry areas.

Elk Island National Park in Alberta preserves both the natural vegetation of the region and this bison herd.

Trees and shrubs grow along streams and near bodies of water. They are not as large as trees in the Cordillera region. Most of these trees are **deciduous**. They lose their leaves and become dormant in winter. New leaves grow in spring when water is more plentiful.

In the far northern parts of the Interior Plains, the winter is cold and the summer is very short. Only small plants, grasses and mosses grow. There are no trees.

# Animal Life

The grasslands, forests and the northern plains are habitats for many animals, birds and other forms of life.

Migratory waterfowl like these ducks travel long distances to spend different seasons in different places.

Deer, antelope, elk, moose and caribou are **herbivores**. They live on grasses, shrubs and other vegetation.

Antelope herds are found in Grasslands National Park.

**Carnivores** are meat-eating animals that hunt other animals. Some carnivores in the southern part of the plains are coyotes, hawks and eagles. Wolves and polar bears live in the north.

Ducks, geese, swans and other waterfowl spend the summer in the northern part of the region. In the autumn, they migrate in huge flocks. They stop in grain fields of the plains and wetlands to feed and rest on their long journey. **Wetlands** are places that are marshy or partly flooded all year round.

# Natural Resources

There are important mineral resources and oil and gas fields below the surface of the Interior Plains. Large amounts of coal and potash are mined in the region. Huge fields of crude oil and natural gas are found far underground. Gas and oil are produced by drilling deep into the Earth.

The Interior Plains produce 90% of Canada's potash. Potash is an important ingredient in fertilizer.

The largest area of farmland in Canada is found in the southern part of the region. The soil is considered **fertile**. It contains a good mixture of materials that grow healthy plants. Cereal grains, such as wheat, oats, barley and rye, grow well on the plains. Cereal grains are all types of grasses whose seeds are used as food.

Grain products and oil and natural gas from the Interior Plains are sold in Canada and around the world.

## Soils

Soils are materials on the surface of the Earth in which plants can grow. They are made of pieces of finely ground rock mixed with decaying plant and animal materials. Plants grow in the top layer, called topsoil.

In most places, soils are only a thin layer on top of the bedrock of the Earth. Soil takes thousands of years to form naturally. That is why soil **erosion** is a problem. When topsoil is carried away by water, wind or ice, or stripped off by machinery, it is a non-renewable resource. It needs thousands of years for new soil to form.

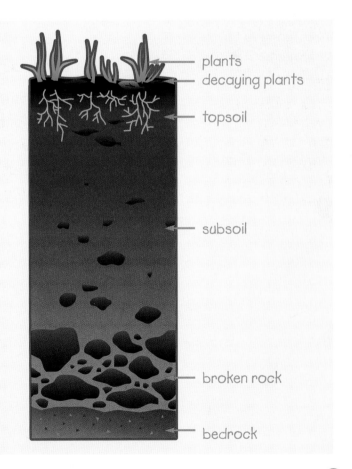

plants
decaying plants
topsoil
subsoil
broken rock
bedrock

# Luke's Concern

I live with *my family* on a farm near Lacombe, Alberta. Most of the wheat in Canada is grown in the southern part of the Interior Plains region. Other types of grain, such as rye, oats and barley, are also grown there.

Many grain farmers use fertilizer and pesticides. They can increase the amount of grain the land will yield. However, pesticides and fertilizer can be washed into streams. They go into the underground water supply.

Some farmers are afraid of damaging the environment. They try to use organic methods. They use natural forms of fertilizer and no pesticides. Unfortunately, these methods do not yield as much grain.

Producing food is important. However, I am concerned about damage to the environment of the Plains.

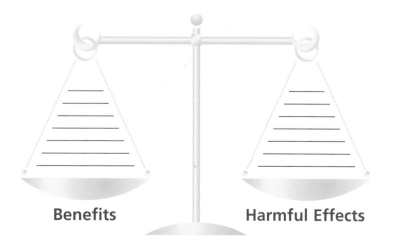

Benefits          Harmful Effects

### Do ◆ Discuss ◆ Discover

1. Brainstorm as many things as you can that come from farms in the Interior Plains.
2. What are "organic" methods of farming? Give an example.
3. With your class, talk about the benefits of using pesticides and fertilizers. Then talk about ways they can harm us and the environment.

# Chapter 3

## Understanding Concepts

1. Draw a region organizer similar to the one you did on page 27 of Chapter 2. Write the title "The Interior Plains" at the top. Use information from this chapter and your notes to fill in every area of the organizer. Put it in your notebook.

2. Identify vocabulary from this chapter to add to the vocabulary section of your notebook. Draw diagrams or sketches to help you remember the words and their meanings.

3. Look at the pictures shown below. Describe what each tells about the Interior Plains region.

## Developing Inquiry/Research and Communication Skills

4. Study the ingredients on three different cereal boxes. List the names of the cereals and the types of grain used in them.

## Developing Map/Globe Skills

5. On an outline map of North America, draw and label the latitude lines from 45° N to 80° N in intervals of 5°. Put this map in your notebook.

## Applying Concepts and Skills in Various Contexts

6. Create a postcard to a friend from the Interior Plains. Show one or more important characteristics of this region. On the back of the card, explain why this image represents the Interior Plains region to you.

## Internet Connection

7. To find out about the famous dinosaur museum in the Interior Plains, go to www.tyrrellmuseum.com

## The Canada Project

1. Find the outline map of Canada you started at the end of Chapter 2. Colour the Interior Plains region. Label the provinces/territories that are in the Interior Plains region. Add important information about the Interior Plains region to your map. (Use the maps on page 28 and inside the front and back covers of the text to help.)

2. Find a special image, or create your own, that gives information and creates a feeling about your province/territory. On the back describe in your own words the foreground, middle ground and background of the picture.

# Chapter 4
# The Arctic Lowlands

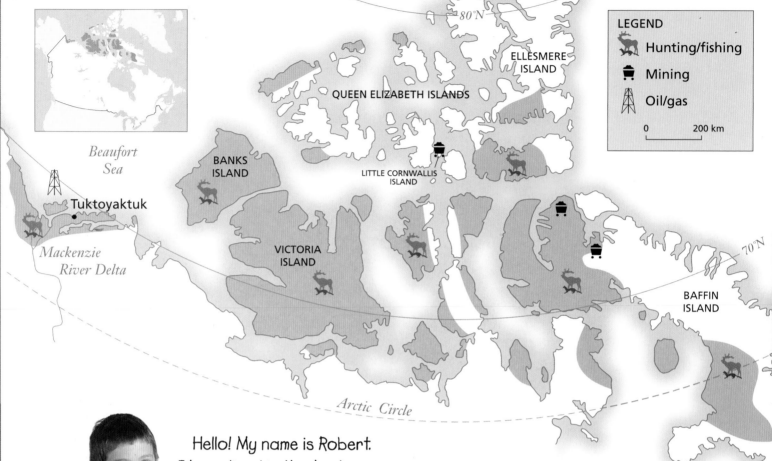

*80°N*

ELLESMERE
ISLAND

QUEEN ELIZABETH ISLANDS

**LEGEND**

Hunting/fishing

Mining

Oil/gas

0    200 km

*Beaufort
Sea*

BANKS
ISLAND

LITTLE CORNWALLIS
ISLAND

Tuktoyaktuk

*Mackenzie
River Delta*

VICTORIA
ISLAND

*70°N*

BAFFIN
ISLAND

*Arctic Circle*

Hello! My name is Robert. I have lived in the Arctic Lowlands for five years. Part of the far northern coast of Canada and many islands in the Arctic Ocean make up this small region. It includes parts of the Yukon Territory, the Northwest Territories and Nunavut. It does not include the mountainous islands at the very top of Canada.

Almost all of the Arctic Lowlands region is found north of the Arctic Circle. The Arctic Circle is at 66 ½° N latitude.

## Focus on Learning

In this chapter you will learn about
- the physical environment of the Arctic Lowlands region
- adaptations of animals to their environment
- interpreting ideas found in songs, sculptures and legends
- notemaking
- how land can be affected by natural resource exploration
- identifying concerns

## Vocabulary

Arctic Circle
Ice Age
permafrost
pingo
sea ice
tundra

barren
treeline
adaptation
non-renewable
  resources

# Physical Features

The Arctic Lowlands are mostly low-lying islands and parts of the northern shore of Canada. About 18 thousand years ago, the temperatures on Earth were much lower. All of this land was covered by glaciers. This period was called an **Ice Age**.

The shoreline is low-lying, but some northern islands have higher elevations.

The Arctic Lowlands are large areas of rock and boggy plains. Soils are thin and not very good for growing plants. Only the surface thaws in summer. The ground below remains frozen all year round. This is called **permafrost**.

In areas with permafrost, you can also see rounded hills called **pingos**. Pingo is an Inuit word for these landforms. Pingos have a core of solid ice. They gradually grow larger as more water freezes onto the ice in the centre of the hill.

These tourists are photographing a large pingo on the delta of the Mackenzie River.

In winter, **sea ice** forms in the salt water of the ocean and the passages between islands, called straits. In summer, the sea ice melts and breaks up into floating sheets of ice called ice floes. Ice floes may be a few metres across or many kilometres across.

Whales need to find breaks in the sea ice to come up to breathe.

These caribou can be seen from a distance because much of the land of the Arctic Lowlands is flat.

# Climate

**Dec. 21**
**0.0 hours**

**Mar. 21**
**12.5 hours**

**June 21**
**24.0 hours**

**Sept. 21**
**12.5 hours**

## Temperature

Summer in the Arctic is brief but sunny. In the middle of the summer, the sun does not set all night long. It rarely gets hot, but summers are warm and skies are clear. It can reach 15° C on a summer day.

Plants like these mountain avens form seeds quickly because the summer is very brief.

The winters are very cold and long. In January, temperatures can reach a low of –45° C. In the middle of the winter, the sun does not come above the horizon at all.

## Precipitation

There is little precipitation in the Arctic Lowlands. Rainfall in summer is not common. Some snow falls in the winter. However, this region gets less snow than most other regions of Canada.

Northern Lights brighten up this dark time. These sheets of light are caused by energy from the sun acting on particles in the air high in the sky.

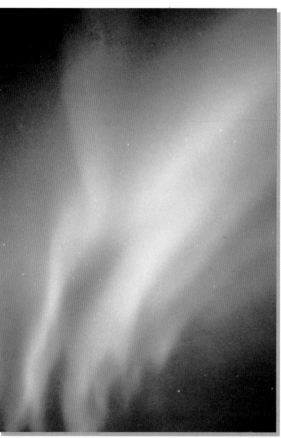

Northern Lights are also known as Aurora Borealis. Moving sheets and bands of light stream across the dark sky.

Houses and clothing must protect people from the extreme cold.

# Vegetation

The physical features and climate of the Arctic Lowlands affect the plants that grow there. Thin soils, cold temperatures, low precipitation, a short summer and permafrost all affect vegetation.

Only small scattered plants, mosses and low-growing shrubs grow in the region. The name for this low Arctic vegetation is tundra. During the long summer days, many small plants produce bright flowers.

Some places are barren. This means they have few living plants. Tundra vegetation grows slowly. If the environment is damaged, plants will take a very long time to grow again.

Tundra is similar to the vegetation above the treeline on high mountains. That is the line past which trees can no longer grow.

This freshly caught Arctic char is lying on tundra vegetation.

# Animal Life

Animals that live here have made adaptations to help them live in the region. That means their bodies have special features that help them survive. Land animals have thick fur. Many have white coats or turn white in winter so that they are difficult to see. Some of the land animals are caribou, musk oxen, polar bears, wolves, Arctic foxes and Arctic hares.

Peary caribou are found only on a few Arctic islands. They are an endangered species.

The ocean waters contain marine animals. Whales, seals and walruses are found there. They have adapted to the cold water and ice by having a thick layer of fat called blubber under their skins. They can swim under the ice. However, they must find holes in the ice or open water to come up to breathe.

Snowy owls hunt for food in the daytime.

Many birds live in the Arctic in summer. Loons, snow geese, snowy owls and ivory gulls nest in the region. They raise their young, and then migrate farther south in the autumn.

## Do ◆ Discuss ◆ Discover

Write answers to these questions in your notebook.

1. What are two ways that the tops of high mountains and the Arctic Lowlands are similar?

2. Why would having a white coat in winter be an advantage for a hare and for a fox?

# The Gift of the Whale

When the Great Spirit created this land, he made many beautiful and good things. He made the sun and the moon and the stars. He made the wide land, white with snow, and the mountains and the ocean. He made fish of all kinds and the many birds. He made the seals and the walrus and the great bears. Then the Great Spirit made the Inupiaq. He had a special love for the people and showed them how to live, using everything around them.

Then after making all this, the Great Spirit decided to make one thing more. This would be the best creation of all. The Great Spirit made this being with great care. It was the Bowhead Whale. It was, indeed, the most beautiful and the finest of the things made by the Great Spirit. As it swam, it flowed through the ocean. It sang as it went, and it was in perfect balance with everything around it.

But the Great Spirit saw something else. He saw that the Inupiaq people needed the Bowhead Whale. Without the whale, it would be hard for them to survive. They needed to eat *muktuk*, the flesh of the whale, to keep warm and healthy during the long, cold nights. They needed its bones to help build their homes. They needed every part of the great whale.

So the Great Spirit gave the Bowhead to the Inupiaq. He gave them a way to hunt it from their boats covered with walrus hide. He made a special time each spring, when the ice of the ocean would break apart to form a road where the whales would swim. In that whale road, the Open Lead, the whales would come to the surface and wait there to be struck by the harpoons of the Inupiaq. They would continue to do so every year as long as the Inupiaq showed respect to the Bowhead, as long as the Inupiaq only took the few whales that they needed in order to survive.

But the Great Spirit decided this also. At that time each year when the Open Lead formed, when the whales came to the surface to be hunted, the Great Spirit made it so that a heavy cloud of thick mist would hang just above the ice, just above the heads of the whales and the Inupiaq. That thick mist would hang there between the sea and the sky. "Though I give you permission to kill my most perfect creation," the Great Spirit said, "I do not wish to watch it."

– a legend of the Inupiaq

## Do ◆ Discuss ◆ Discover

1. As a class, discuss the following:
   a) What is a legend?
   b) What special gift did the Great Spirit give the Inupiaq?
   c) What made this gift special?
   d) How did they use the Bowhead whale?
   e) What tools did the Great Spirit give the Inupiaq to help them hunt the whales?
   f) How did the Great Spirit help the whales?
   g) Why should we protect the Bowhead whales?

# Arctic Lowlands Arts

## The Earth and the People

The Earth was here before the
  people.
The very first people
Came out of the ground.
Everything came from the
  ground,
Even caribou.
Children once grew
Out of the ground
Just as flowers do.
Women out wandering found
  them sprawling on the grass
And took them home and nursed
  them.
That way people multiplied.

This land of ours
Has become habitable
Because we came here
And learned how to hunt.

  – traditional Inuit song

Bessie Hikomak
and Martina
Anavilok with
Bessie's sealskin
tapestry

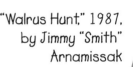

"Walrus Hunt," 1987,
by Jimmy "Smith"
Arnamissak

## Do ◆ Discuss ◆ Discover

1. Discuss with your small group members the things the songwriter says about the Earth. Share your group's thoughts with the rest of the class. Then answer this question in your notebook.

   a) How does the songwriter guide you to understand that the Earth was the source of life?

2. Discuss how the sculpture and tapestry represent life in the Arctic Lowlands.

3. Draw a picture showing your favourite part of this song or create a design for a sculpture or tapestry that represents the Arctic Lowlands. (This could go in your project scrapbook or shoebox, or in your notebook.)

# Horns and Paws

## Do ◆ Discuss ◆ Discover

Do the following questions in groups of three:

1. Use a variety of sources (books, Internet, encyclopedia) to help you name the animals represented by the shadows above.
2. Discuss what you know about the animals in the Arctic.
3. Using an organizer (see page 12), compare them with what you have learned about animals in other parts of Canada. Put this in your notebook.

## Hands On!

Work by yourself to create an animal track.

You will need

- self-hardening clay
- waxed paper
- a carving tool
- picture of a paw or hoof print
- some dark paint

1. Locate a picture of a paw or hoof print.
2. Cover your desk with waxed paper before beginning.
3. Form a small ball of clay, and then flatten it to about 2 cm thick.
4. Study the picture of the paw or hoof print. It is your guide to what the print should look like. Some areas will be more indented than others.
5. Carve into the clay to make a hollowed-out impression of the paw or hoof print.
6. Set the print to one side overnight to harden.
7. Use a small amount of dark paint to emphasize the print.
8. Label your print.

# Natural Resources

The Arctic Lowlands region has few renewable resources other than its animal life. There is no farmland or forest. The animals and sea life provide important food and clothing resources for the people who live there. Some products are sold outside the region.

The region has important **non-renewable** resources, such as zinc, lead, oil, natural gas and coal. These are called non-renewable because they disappear after being used.

Lead and zinc are mined on Little Cornwallis Island and the north end of Baffin Island in Nunavut.

The Polaris mine on Little Cornwallis Island is the most northerly mine in the world!

A large oil field lies below the Beaufort Sea and the Mackenzie River delta of the Northwest Territories. Oil companies have been exploring and drilling test wells in the Mackenzie Delta and offshore in the Beaufort Sea since the 1970s.

The cost of producing and transporting oil and gas to markets farther south is very high. There is still no large production of oil and gas in this part of the region.

Some products from the region besides minerals are sold elsewhere in Canada and the world. These include furs, frozen fish such as Arctic char, and works of art such as soapstone sculptures.

The Arctic char is similar to the salmon. These fish are a source of food and income for people in the region.

Soapstone is an easily carved rock found in many places in Canada, including the far North. Inuit artists have created soapstone sculptures that have been sold around the world.

Inuit sculptures usually show the relationship between the people and the animals of the region.

# Note-making

Your notebook is a place to keep information about what you have studied in class. You may also include notes made when doing research or reading for information. Making notes will help you remember. You can use your notes to study for tests or prepare for projects. Notes can be in different forms, such as

- point form notes (main topics and related details)
- notes in a chart or organizer
- notes in a web, to show connections between ideas
- pictures, diagrams, timelines

## Organizing Your Notes

1. Put the date at the top of each new set of notes.

2. Give each day's work a title. If you used the textbook, write the page number with your notes.

3. Underline the title and the date with a coloured pencil and ruler.

4. Make brief notes but include all of the important topics and some important details about the topics.

## Writing Point Form Notes

1. Point form notes don't need to be sentences, just key phrases.

2. Reread the passage. Use the main idea as a title.

3. List the topic of each paragraph. These are the main ideas of the passage.

4. Under each topic, list key words and supporting details from the paragraph.

5. You may want to draw pictures beside each topic to remind you.

6. Underline or highlight key words and definitions.

**Example**

Natural Resources (Arctic Lowlands)
- renewable resources
  - few renewable resources
  - no farmland and forests
  - animal and sea life
- non-renewable resources
  - zinc, lead, oil, natural gas, coal
  - <u>non-renewable means cannot grow again</u>
- minerals and oil
  - lead and zinc mined
  - oil exploration
- other products
  - furs, fish, soapstone art

# Arctic Oil and Gas Exploration

Oil and gas fields are found under both the land and the oceans of the world. Drilling for oil and gas in the Arctic Lowlands presents many challenges. Some challenges are sea ice, the storms, the cold, the remote location and the sensitive environment.

Several kinds of offshore drilling rigs have been developed. Some platforms float. Some are built on long pillars or artificial islands. Drill ships with very strong hulls have been used in some deep-water areas.

Exploration wells are drilled to locate sources of oil and gas.

The environment of the Mackenzie River delta is fragile and easily damaged. Heat from buildings, machinery and people raise the temperature of the ground. When the permafrost begins to melt underneath, the ground turns into bog. Equipment and buildings can sink below the surface.

Most Arctic exploration is done far away from populated places. Welders, mechanics, electricians, engineers and drilling specialists stay at a well site for long periods. Cooks, firefighters, computer technicians and helicopter pilots also live on the site. It is like working on a ship far from shore.

Oil and gas workers earn extra money for working in harsh conditions.

Even though the companies make sure that they work carefully, oil spills are possible. It is very difficult to clean up a spill in such a severe climate. The people in the area hope that the oil companies will never have to test their disaster plans.

Supplies are transported by air on cargo planes.

## Do ◆ Discuss ◆ Discover

1. In your notebook, write point form notes about this passage about Arctic oil and gas exploration.

2. Look on page 46 at the list of different ways of making notes. What kinds of information about Arctic oil and gas drilling would you record on a web or chart? Share your ideas with one other student and then complete either a web or a chart to put in your notebook.

# Robert's Concern

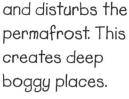

My family and I live in Tuktoyaktuk, Northwest Territories. My father works for a company that drills for oil. Many people want the oil company here because the company promised us new roads, more business and a better airport.

and disturbs the permafrost. This creates deep boggy places.

When plants in this environment die, it is a very long time before others grow. If the land or ocean is polluted, many animals, birds and fish die. Some kinds, like musk oxen, are found only in the Arctic. If their habitat changes, they will be endangered.

People who live here depend on the environment for food. As the community changes and the population increases, there are more needs to be met. More food and products are imported. More energy is used to heat buildings and run machinery. More waste and garbage are produced. Garbage cannot be buried because of the permafrost. It is a hazard for the birds and wildlife of the region.

Travel on the tundra creates deep ruts in summer. It kills plants

I am concerned that the changes in the community will cause permanent changes in the environment. We need to think about how to prevent this.

## Do ◆ Discuss ◆ Discover

1. Discuss why plants grow so slowly in this region. Review the Physical Features, Climate and Vegetation sections of this chapter.
2. What would be three things you would tell new people to the area about the environment in the Arctic Lowlands to help protect it?

# Chapter 4

## Understanding Concepts

1. Draw a region organizer similar to the one you did on page 37 of Chapter 3. Write the title "The Arctic Lowlands" at the top. Using information from this chapter and your notes, fill in every area of the organizer. Put it in your notebook.

2. Identify vocabulary from this chapter to add to the vocabulary section of your notebook. Draw diagrams or sketches to help you remember the words and their meanings.

3. Explain in a paragraph how animals have adapted to the climate of the Arctic Lowlands.

## Developing Inquiry/Research and Communication Skills

4. Research the musk ox. Follow the research model on page 14. Choose a form of note-making and write notes about the musk ox. (This could go in your scrapbook or shoebox.)

## Developing Map/Globe Skills

5. On an outline of a globe, draw and label the Arctic Circle (66½° N latitude). Create your own pictorial symbols to show the hours of daylight in all four seasons at the Arctic Circle.

## Applying Concepts and Skills in Various Contexts

6. Describe in two paragraphs how your daily schedule might change if it were daylight for 23 hours a day where you live.

## Internet Connection

7. Visit the website www.wwfcanada.org to view the section called Critter of the Month. Create point form notes about that animal.

## The Canada Project

1. Find the outline map of Canada you started at the end of Chapter 2. Colour the Arctic Lowlands region. Label the provinces/territories that are in the region. Add important information about the Arctic Lowlands region to your map. (Use the maps on page 38 and inside the front and back covers of the text to help.)

2. Create a sculpture or locate a small figurine of one animal that lives in your province or territory to put in your shoebox.

3. Research a legend, poem or song from your province/territory to put in your scrapbook or shoebox. Add your own illustrations to make it interesting and fun.

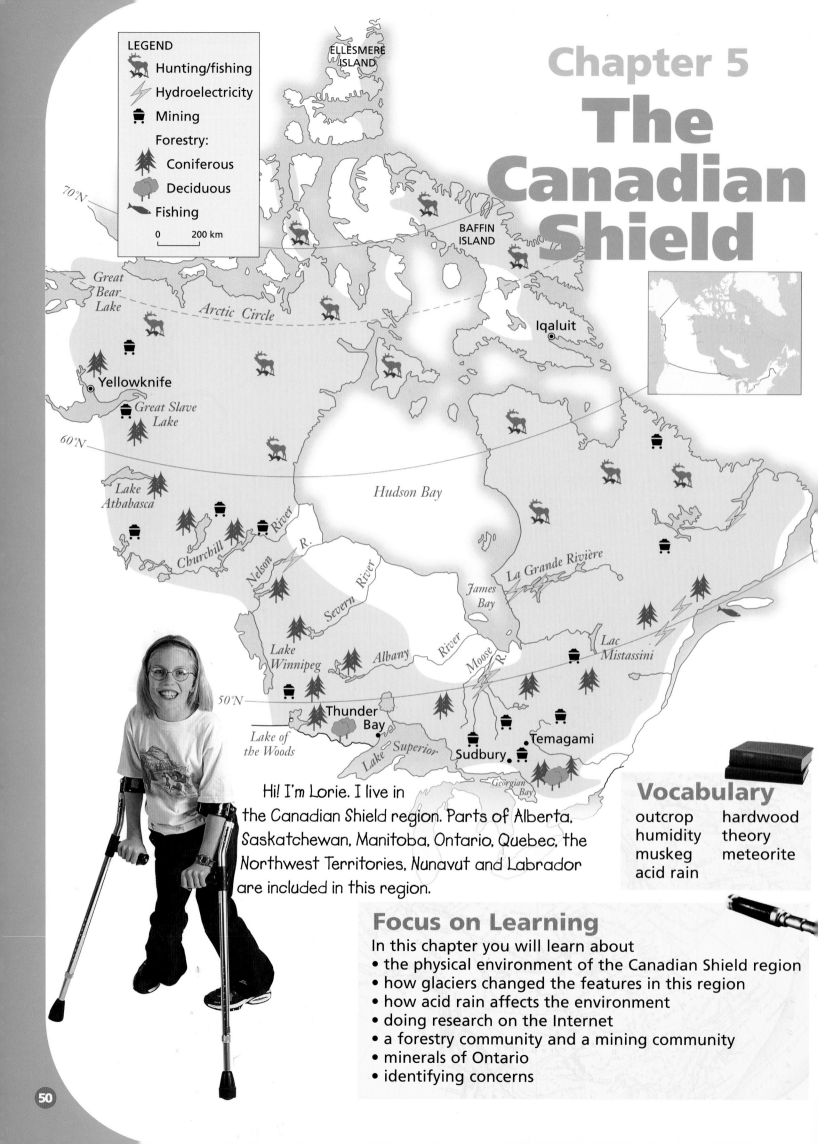

**LEGEND**

🦌 Hunting/fishing
⚡ Hydroelectricity
⛏ Mining

Forestry:
🌲 Coniferous
🌳 Deciduous
🐟 Fishing

0 ___ 200 km

ELLESMERE ISLAND

BAFFIN ISLAND

70°N

60°N

50°N

Great Bear Lake

Arctic Circle

Yellowknife

Great Slave Lake

Lake Athabasca

Churchill River

Nelson R.

Severn River

Lake Winnipeg

Lake of the Woods

Thunder Bay

Lake Superior

Hudson Bay

James Bay

Albany River

Moose R.

Georgian Bay

Sudbury

Temagami

Iqaluit

La Grande Rivière

Lac Mistassini

# Chapter 5
# The Canadian Shield

Hi! I'm Lorie. I live in the Canadian Shield region. Parts of Alberta, Saskatchewan, Manitoba, Ontario, Quebec, the Northwest Territories, Nunavut and Labrador are included in this region.

## Vocabulary

outcrop        hardwood
humidity       theory
muskeg         meteorite
acid rain

## Focus on Learning

In this chapter you will learn about
• the physical environment of the Canadian Shield region
• how glaciers changed the features in this region
• how acid rain affects the environment
• doing research on the Internet
• a forestry community and a mining community
• minerals of Ontario
• identifying concerns

# Physical Features

The Canadian Shield covers about half of Canada. The landforms are similar everywhere in the region. It has rocky hills and thousands of lakes, rivers, streams and marshes. The layer of soil over rock is thin in most places. Many **outcrops** of bare rock show through it.

The glaciers of the Ice Age spread across this region. The weight of the ice scraped the surface of the rocky hills. In many places you can see long scratches on the rock. These were made when stones frozen in the ice of a glacier dragged across the bedrock.

Loose rock and soil were pushed and dragged great distances. When the glaciers melted and retreated, the rock and soil were left behind, creating hills and gravel beds.

Many river systems of the Canadian Shield flow towards Hudson Bay. Other rivers flow into the Great Lakes and St. Lawrence River system, which flows to the Atlantic Ocean.

First Snow, North Shore of Lake Superior by Lawren S. Harris

Rocky outcrops, lakes and coniferous trees are typical of the Canadian Shield.

## Do ◆ Discuss ◆ Discover

1. With a partner, carefully examine the painting *First Snow, North Shore of Lake Superior* by Lawren S. Harris.
   a) What do you see in the foreground, middle ground and background?
   b) What seems to be the most important thing in the painting?
   c) What natural thing do you think scratched the rocks? How?
   d) What season do you associate with those colours?
   e) What do you think this painting says about what this region is like?

2. On your own, imitate the style of the painting. Paint a picture of your neighbourhood during the same season. Put this in your notebook.

# Glacier Simulation

Materials needed:

- 20 x 30 x 10 cm cake pan
- 1 cm of sand in a large flat baking tray (or use a sand table)
    - handful of very cold pebbles
    - water

1. Put 5 cm of water in the cake pan and freeze it. Put the pebbles in the freezer to get cold.

2. Remove the sheet of ice from the cake pan. Place the cold pebbles on top of the sand in the tray and place the sheet of ice on top. Press down on the ice, the pebbles and the sand. Let the ice sit for a while. Notice that sand and pebbles have attached to the bottom of the ice, making the bottom surface bumpy and sandy.

3. Slide the ice sheet slowly along the sand. Notice that a mound of sand is pushed ahead of the ice sheet. Notice the trench that the ice sheet carves as it moves. Notice the grooves that the pebbles scratch on the sandy surface. Push the ice sheet from one end of the tray of sand to the other.

4. Leave the ice sitting on the sand to melt. (Continue with the next part of this chapter.)

5. Every half hour, observe the progress of the melting ice. As the ice melts, observe that the material pushed by the ice sheet is left behind. It marks the glacier's farthest point of advance. Observe that the pebbles dragged underneath the ice sheet are deposited along the way.

6. Record your observations in writing and a diagram and put them in your notebook.

# Climate

Winters in the Canadian Shield are cold. In the far north, there is less snow. In the southern part, snowfall can be very heavy.

A winter day in the northern Canadian Shield

Early winter on the shore of Lake Superior

Summers in the far north are similar to the Arctic Lowlands. They are brief but the days are very long. Farther south the summer is warmer and more humid. **Humidity** is the amount of water vapour in the air. The southern areas of the Canadian Shield get up to 1600 mm of precipitation every year. Much of it falls as snow, but rain in the summer is also common.

# Vegetation

The northern part of the area has tundra vegetation. There are small plants, mosses and low-growing shrubs. Rocky areas are barren. Farther south, scattered coniferous trees and shrubs grow. In places where there is more soil, there are forests of coniferous trees.

Between the rocky hills are boggy wetlands called **muskeg**. Muskeg is formed as living and dead vegetation gradually fills in lakes.

Muskeg, with coniferous trees

The forests that grow farthest south in the region are mixed deciduous and coniferous trees.

In autumn the deciduous trees turn yellow or red and the coniferous trees remain dark green.

Many trees are being killed by acid rain. **Acid rain** is formed when pollution in the air mixes with rain. This harmful rain slowly destroys things on which it falls. For example, sugar maple is a valuable tree grown in part of this region. Mature sugar maple woods are being killed by acid rain. They will only regrow if there is no more acid rain. New trees will need many years to mature.

# Acid Rain

Factories and automobiles produce smoke that contains harmful chemicals. Smelters for processing minerals such as nickel from ore create a lot of pollution. So do coal-burning power plants.

Some pollution falls as dry dust. It can damage soil, water, vegetation and anything else it lands on.

Some chemicals in the air come into contact with cloud moisture and dissolve, forming acids. Raindrops and snowflakes also fall through smoke and air pollution and form acids.

Acid rain has an effect on everything it touches. It can crumble the bricks of a building. That shows how strong the chemicals must be!

Many industries are trying to reduce the amount of air pollution they create. Car engines are being designed better. One way we can help reduce acid rain is by not wasting electrical power and heat. Another way is to use our automobiles less.

Harmful chemicals from factories and automobiles float high and mix with the air. Winds may carry the smoke great distances from where it was produced.

The acid rain and snow fall to Earth. They pollute rivers and lakes, killing fish and plants. Pollution also falls on trees and plants, cities, bridges, cars and statues.

For more information on acid rain, visit www.ec.gc.ca/acidrain/acidfact.html

# Animal Life

Many types of animals live on the Canadian Shield. Some examples are woodland caribou, wolves and foxes. In the forests, moose and deer are common.

Many fur-bearing animals make their homes in this region. Black bears, beavers, pine martens, minks, foxes, lynx and muskrats are some examples. They grow heavy warm coats as an adaptation to the winter cold.

Freshwater fish are plentiful in the lakes and rivers. Lake trout, bass, perch, pickerel and whitefish are common freshwater fish. Fish grow very large because there is little commercial fishing. Fly-in sport fishing is an industry that takes advantage of the unspoiled environment and plentiful fish.

# Doing Research on the Internet

The Internet is a powerful research tool. Do Internet research work at school with the guidance of your teacher or at home with your parents. To research on the Internet, you need to learn how to properly use a search engine.

1. Get on the Internet.

2. Locate the search engine. Two common ones are Yahooligans or Google. Usually your Internet menu bar will have a button called Search.

3. You need to define your search. Type a key word to direct the search engine. For example: Ontario, Canada.

4. Notice the number of entries. You need to narrow the search.

5. Choose a more specific entry. For example, begin a new search for a place in Ontario, such as a town or city.

6. Notice the number of entries. There should be fewer.

7. Read the entries to find one that you think will be useful. Notice the web address. If it ends with .ca, it is an address in Canada. If it ends with .on.ca, it is an address in Ontario.

8. Be sure to keep a record of where you find information on the Internet. Write the web address in your notes and add the date you visited it.

# Natural Resources

The Canadian Shield is a region rich with natural resources. Both softwood and **hardwood** are harvested from the forests. Softwood from coniferous forests is used for pulp, paper and lumber for construction. Hardwood is used for building furniture, cabinets and wall panelling. Maple, oak, birch and walnut are all valued for their beautiful, strong wood.

Many rivers of the region are used to make hydroelectricity. Some hydroelectric power is sold to other regions.

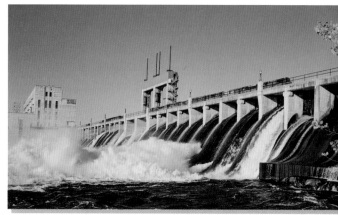

A hydroelectric power plant at Seven Sisters Falls on the Winnipeg River produces electricity used in the Interior Plains Region.

Sawmills cut trees into lumber for construction materials.

Mining is one of the most important industries in this region. Minerals found in the Canadian Shield include copper, iron, lead, nickel, gold, silver, uranium and zinc. In 1991, a mining company discovered diamonds just east of Great Bear Lake, Northwest Territories.

Some mines are underground. Others, like this one, are surface mines, sometimes called open-pit mines.

Mine workers need to be strong and willing to work underground in uncomfortable conditions.

## Do ◆ Discuss ◆ Discover

1. Use the guideline on the previous page to plan an Internet search for information about one resource of the Canadian Shield that is found in Ontario. What key words would you use? How would you narrow the search if you did not find something suitable the first time?

# Temagami—a Forestry Community

Temagami is a northern Ontario township with fewer than 1000 people. It is 100 km north of North Bay. The name of the township is pronounced "Te-MAWG-a-mee." It is an Ojibway word meaning "deep water by the shore." The township is surrounded by pine forests, clear waters and bountiful fish and wildlife.

Temagami is set amidst the lakes and trees of the Canadian Shield.

Trails and boardwalks through wetlands allow visitors to see the environment up close.

Temagami has been known for outdoor and wilderness recreation for over 100 years. Cottages, fishing and hunting lodges, and hotels dot the area. One-third of the last surviving ancient white and red pine forest in the world is found around Temagami. There are 25 km of trails through old uncut forests.

The Temagami area was first logged in the 1920s and 1930s. There are interesting places for visitors to learn about the early lumbering industry. Old camps, sawmills, log chutes and fire towers can be visited.

There is a historic fire tower on a hill above Temagami. Forest rangers watched from the tower for forest fires. If danger was spotted, they directed fire crews to the location. The fire tower is now a site for tourists to visit.

The fire tower on the hill is a local landmark.

## Visit Temagami

1. a)  Do an Internet search for Temagami, Ontario, to find out more about the community.
   b)  You can take a virtual tour of the firetower on the site www.twp.temagami.on.ca

## Do ◆ Discuss ◆ Discover

1.  Imagine you are a forest ranger. Write a letter to your family or a friend about what being a forest ranger might be like.

# Minerals of Ontario

The Canadian Shield covers two-thirds of Ontario. Mining has been important to Ontario since the early 1800s. Ontario's first gold rush took place near the town of Madoc in 1866.

Today, Ontario is one of the world's top 10 mineral producers. It produces more than 30 different minerals. Eighty per cent of Ontario's mineral production is sold around the world.

Nickel, gold, copper, uranium, zinc, platinum, cobalt and silver are mined in Ontario. Many towns in northern Ontario were built because of mining activities.

## A Theory about Some Minerals

Scientists have developed theories about why this area is so rich in minerals. Theories are ideas that people think could be true because there is lots of evidence to support them, but they have not been proven.

One theory is that some of the minerals came from meteorites. Meteorites are rocks from outer space that crash into the Earth. They think the meteorites may have contained minerals we are now mining. The impact of a meteorite would form a huge circular hollow, like the craters on the surface of the moon. The mineral ores would be melted in the impact and then cool.

Amethyst is the official mineral of the province of Ontario. This piece was found near Thunder Bay.

## Do ◆ Discuss ◆ Discover

Choose one of the following two activities to complete with a partner.

1. a) Locate and then place these mining towns and cities on a map of Ontario: Red Lake, Hemlo, Wawa, Elliot Lake, Timmins, Manitouwadge, Sudbury and Kirkland Lake.

   b) Research the minerals mined near these towns and cities.

   c) Decide which symbols you could use to represent the minerals mined in those locations.

   d) Create a legend of symbols for your map and add the symbols beside the locations on your map.

2. a) Research two theories of why the Sudbury area is so rich in minerals. If you use the Internet, begin your search using these key words:

   Meteorite, Sudbury Basin
   Magma, Sudbury Basin

   b) Decide which theory is more interesting to you. Explain your reasons in a paragraph and put it in your notebook.

# Sudbury—a Mining Community

The city of Sudbury sits in a huge oval-shaped dent in the rocky Canadian Shield. This basin is 60 km by 27 km. It holds one of the Earth's richest known deposits of nickel and copper. Mining is a $3 billion-a-year business for Sudbury. One of the world's largest deposits of nickel is found there.

was eroded. Blackened bare rock outcrops with scattered, unhealthy plants surrounded Sudbury. Many people said it looked like the surface of the moon!

Workers in iron and steel industries must wear protective clothing because of the extreme temperatures.

The people of Sudbury have worked with the mining industry to bring the region back to life. Over the past two decades, people have planted more than 5 million trees. Today weather records show that air pollution levels in Sudbury are lower than in Toronto or Hamilton. The United Nations recently honoured the Region of Sudbury for its land-recovery program.

The Big Nickel is a replica of a Canadian five cent piece 9 metres high and 61 centimetres thick!

Mining and processing of minerals have created many jobs for people. Sudbury is a centre of government, business, education, health care and services.

The Big Nickel mine has guided tours.

Sudbury is the largest city in northeast Ontario.

Industries brought wealth but created problems for the region. Soils became polluted and topsoil

## Visit Sudbury

1. If you can visit Sudbury, go 20 metres underground at the Big Nickel Mine to find out how it feels to be a miner. See exhibits of different mining methods. View an emergency refuge station, many different pieces of mining equipment, an underground garden and the only underground mailbox in Canada!

## Do ◆ Discuss ◆ Discover

1. Write an imaginary postcard from Sudbury to put in the only underground mailbox in Canada. Draw your own picture on the front and write a message to a friend on the back.

# Lorie's Concern

My father works with the regional Conservation Authority. He says that Sudbury looks much better than it used to.

For a long time, we did not pay attention to how the land around us was affected. Then people began to notice that very few plants and fish lived in the lake. The area looked bad. Trees had died, and other vegetation looked sick.

My father and the people who lived here made sure that the mining companies started to pay attention. Soon they were building taller smokestacks to carry away the smoke. Efforts were made to clean the water and the soil. People worked together to replant grasses, shrubs and trees.

We are proud of our city. However, we are concerned that the same mistakes not be made in the future. We must not forget about what the environment needs to be healthy.

**IN THE PAST**

**PRESENT DAY**

## Do ◆ Discuss ◆ Discover

1. Look at the pictures on this page. Discuss the differences you see.

2. Discuss what ideas you get from the photos that demonstrate what people can do to improve their environment.

## Understanding Concepts

1. Draw a region organizer similar to the one you did on page 49 of Chapter 4. Write the title "The Canadian Shield" at the top. Using information from this chapter and your notes, fill in every area of the organizer. Put it in your notebook.

2. Identify vocabulary from this chapter to add to the vocabulary section of your notebook. Draw diagrams or sketches to help you remember the words and their meanings.

3. Explain in your own words how acid rain is formed. Add pictures or illustrations to make your explanation very clear.

## Developing Inquiry/Research and Communication Skills

4. Research how acid rain affects the water cycle. Follow the research model on page 14. In your notebook, draw a diagram of the water cycle. In your own words, describe the harmful effects of acid rain.

## Developing Map/Globe Skills

5. On an outline map of the Canadian Shield, label the different forests found in this region. Include all necessary parts of a map.

## Applying Concepts and Skills in Various Contexts

6. On the weekend, go for a walk with your family to a local park or conservation area. Find an interesting rock. Identify the type of rock. Give it a name and create a history for it. Design a background with the perfect scenery for your rock.

## Internet Connection

7. Visit the website www.nrcan.gc.ca/ communications/nrcat-rnchat/. Go to Information and then click Our Hidden Treasures. Read each of the sections and create a list of products and jobs that the mining industry provides for Canadian people.

## The Canada Project

1. Find the outline map of Canada you started at the end of Chapter 2. Colour the Canadian Shield region. Label the provinces/territories that are in the region. Add important information about the Canadian Shield region to your map. (Use the maps on page 50 and inside the front and back covers of the text to help.)

2. Create a collage of minerals found in your province/territory. Label each mineral. Try to locate actual samples of the minerals. Put your collage in your scrapbook or shoebox.

# Chapter 6
# The Hudson Bay Lowlands

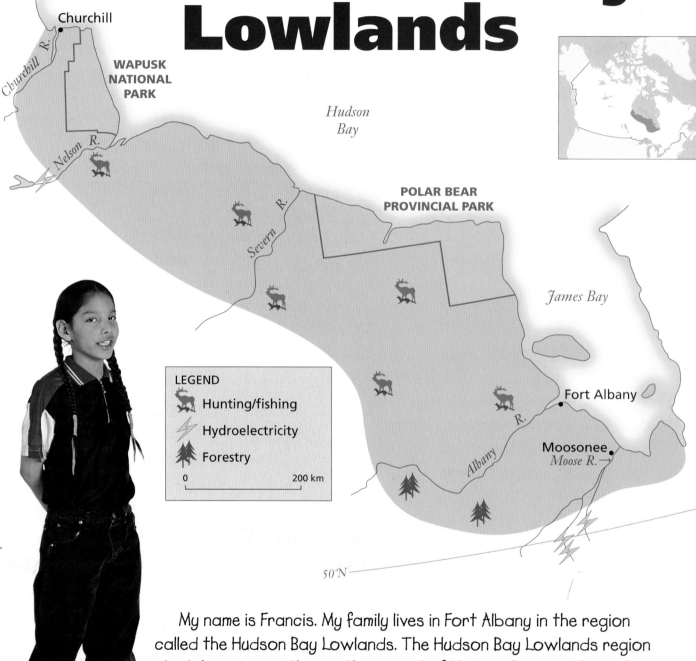

Churchill

**WAPUSK NATIONAL PARK**

*Churchill R.*

*Nelson R.*

*Hudson Bay*

*Severn R.*

**POLAR BEAR PROVINCIAL PARK**

*James Bay*

Fort Albany

Moosonee

*Moose R.* →

*Albany R.*

*50°N*

LEGEND
- Hunting/fishing
- Hydroelectricity
- Forestry

0      200 km

My name is Francis. My family lives in Fort Albany in the region called the Hudson Bay Lowlands. The Hudson Bay Lowlands region stretches around the southern part of Hudson Bay and James Bay. It includes parts of Manitoba, northern Ontario and Quebec.

## Vocabulary

peat      eco-tourism
breed      conservation

## Focus on Learning
In this chapter you will learn about
- the physical environment of the Hudson Bay Lowlands region
- a hunting and fishing community
- identifying concerns

# Physical Features

This region is a large plain with a long coastline. It is one of the flattest parts of Canada. Once it was part of Hudson Bay. As the huge Ice Age glaciers retreated, the level of the land rose. This flat land was exposed and began to dry. However, it is so near to sea level that it is marshy and water does not drain away.

Many rivers flow through the lowlands into Hudson Bay and James Bay. When the snow is melting on the Canadian Shield and Interior Plains, this low-lying area floods. Wetlands are lands that are marshy or flooded most of the time.

Much of the region has permafrost. The surface of the land melts in summer and vegetation grows, but the ground remains frozen underneath. The permafrost is another reason why water does not drain away easily.

The Hudson Bay Lowlands region is the world's largest wetland area, approximately 300 000 square kilometres.

Although the ice melts along the shore of Hudson Bay these waters are never completely free of sea ice.

The Hudson Bay Lowlands region is very flat. The scattered rocks here were dropped by a melting glacier.

## Hands On!

Try this simple experiment to see how the Hudson Bay Lowlands formed after the glaciers retreated.

You will need

- large rectangular baking pan
- wooden board smaller than the pan
- two small stones (about 2 cm)
- water
- a weight (for example, a 500 gram stone or a large block of ice)

1. Fill the pan half full with water. Put the small stones on the bottom against one edge. Float the board on top of the water with one end over the small stones. Place the weight on the other end of the board. Notice that it sinks to the bottom of the pan. The water reaches up over part of the board.

2. Gradually slide the weight towards the end resting on the stones. Notice what happens to the board. Record your observations in your notebook. Share these observations with two other students.

# Climate

The Hudson Bay Lowlands region has long, cold winters and short, warm summers.

This region has long, cold winters.

Precipitation is moderate. Most of it falls as snow in winter. The climate is very similar to that of the northern part of the Canadian Shield.

Tundra vegetation blooms brightly in the short summer.

The vegetation in the southwestern part of the region is more like the Canadian Shield, with coniferous trees and muskeg.

# Vegetation

The coastline of Hudson Bay and James Bay contains long marshes. Reeds and grasses of various kinds grow there.

Reeds and other wetland plants grow near the shore.

The northern part of the region is most like tundra. South of the treeline, there are scattered coniferous trees and some types of deciduous trees. Dense forests of white spruce, balsam fir, aspen and balsam poplar, and white birch grow in the southwestern part of this region.

Black spruce and tamarack grow in the muskeg. Up to 85 percent of the region is muskeg or peat-forming wetland. **Peat** is a deep layer of decaying plant life formed in wet conditions. It is not soil because it contains little sand or other minerals.

### Do ◆ Discuss ◆ Discover

1. a) Look at the map inside the front cover of the book. Estimate the latitude of the part of the region farthest north and the part farthest south.

   b) Discuss how these differences in latitude likely affect the climate and the vegetation.

# Animal Life

Many kinds of fish, birds and animals live and **breed** in the Hudson Bay Lowlands. Birds lay and hatch eggs. Animals give birth and raise their young in the wetlands and forests.

Some of Canada's largest groups of snow geese and Canada geese nest along the coast. Brant geese, whistling swans, eider and merganser ducks, loons, northern phalarope and many kinds of shorebirds also nest in the Lowlands.

Huge flocks of Canada geese live in the wetlands through the summer.

Caribou are found along the coastline in summer. They move inland among the forests in the winter. Many other Arctic mammals live there, such as Arctic foxes, lemmings, the short-tailed weasel and Arctic hares. This region also has a large seal and walrus population.

Polar bears spend most of the winter on the sea. They mainly eat seals. They come to shore in spring. Bears dig earth dens to stay cool in summer. In early winter they make snow dens to wait for the new cubs to be born, until the sea ice forms. Polar bears may go without eating from four to seven months while on shore.

Polar Bear Provincial Park in northern Ontario along the coast of Hudson Bay and Wapusk National Park in Manitoba are both protected places where polar bears live and breed.

Global warming is causing a dangerous situation for the bears. Sometimes the sea ice does not form close to shore. The bears may be trapped on land, far from their main supply of food—the seals. If the winter stays warm, some bears may starve.

The Arctic fox has a heavy white coat in winter. In summer they are a grey colour.

## Do ◆ Discuss ◆ Discover

1. In a short paragraph, explain why the breeding grounds of migratory birds are important.

2. a) What is the purpose of national and provincial parks? Which national or provincial park is nearest to your home?

   b) Why do you think Polar Bear Provincial Park was chosen to be a protected environment?

# Natural Resources

The Hudson Bay Lowlands have no developed mineral reserves or oil and gas wells. It is possible that oil or gas may be found there one day. Underneath Hudson Bay there are layers of rock that are often associated with oil and gas fields.

There are several hydroelectric dams on rivers flowing into Hudson Bay and James Bay. Two large projects are found on the Nelson River in Manitoba and a tributary of the Moose River in Ontario.

This hydroelectric project on the Nelson River uses the force of the water to create electricity.

The big lens on this camera is used to take pictures of distant birds and animals.

Soils of the region are not suitable for agriculture. Most people depend on hunting and fishing for some of their food. Most other supplies arrive by airplane or ship. Hunting, fishing and trapping for furs are part of the way of life of many people in the region.

Parts of the area are known for sports hunting and fishing. **Eco-tourism** is growing in popularity. Eco-tourists are visitors who come to see the animal and bird life, natural vegetation and landforms of the region.

From the observation tower, people can see for long distances across the flat tundra. These caribou pay no attention to the watchers.

First Nations guides accompany most tours. They know the region better than anyone. They make sure that **conservation** rules are followed. Conservation means taking care of the environment.

These visitors are watching polar bears from the safety of a tundra buggy.

## Do ◆ Discuss ◆ Discover

1. In a small group, discuss where the electricity from the hydroelectric projects may go.
2. What features of the region where you live might be interesting to an eco-tourist?
3. Discuss why supplies are brought in by airplane or ship.

# Fort Albany – A Hunting and Fishing Community

Fort Albany is a First Nations hunting and fishing community of about 850 people. It is located on the shore of James Bay at the mouth of the Albany River.

The best way to get to Fort Albany is by air.

A winter road connects the community to Moosonee, 128 km to the southeast. It is only open from January until early May. There is passenger, mail and freight service to Fort Albany every day by air.

A barge service brings supplies from the south twice each summer.

People in Fort Albany use motor boats and canoes for hunting, fishing and trapping in summer. Skidoos are the most common way of getting around the community in winter.

Wildlife is plentiful. There are geese, ducks, moose, caribou, bear, beaver, grouse, partridge, foxes and other small animals in the region. Whitefish, trout, northern pike, pickerel and other freshwater fish are found in the rivers and lakes. It is a wonderful place to live if you love to fish!

Many people in Fort Albany are bilingual in Cree and English. Cree is taught in school, and students also learn traditional ways of making crafts. In spring, students get a two-week "hunt break" to take part in goose hunting. A family feast of *niska* (goose) is held at the end of the break.

A new school is being built to replace the old school.

## Visit Fort Albany

1. Imagine you are travelling to Fort Albany on the summer supply barge. Describe what you see on shore as the barge travels slowly up the James Bay coast.

# Francis's Concern

My dad works for the Department of the Environment. He tries to make sure that the people who live in this region and visit here treat the land and its resources properly. He thinks it is important to keep the environment healthy. Both animals and humans need to live here together.

He has been going to meetings about the changes in the environment that can be caused by hydroelectric developments.

Large construction projects such as dams disturb the environment. The vegetation is removed, so mud washes into the river. This changes the habitats of fish, birds and animals.

Huge numbers of waterbirds breed and nest in the wetlands of the region. If their habitat changes, the number of birds will decline.

I am concerned that projects such as hydroelectric dams must be carefully planned because of their effect on the environment.

### Do ◆ Discuss ◆ Discover

1. a) Discuss the importance of suitable nesting and breeding areas for birds and animals that are in this region.
   b) Brainstorm possible questions you would ask at a construction planning meeting in this region.

# Chapter 6

## Understanding Concepts

1. Draw a region organizer similar to the one you did on page 61 of Chapter 5. Write the title "The Hudson Bay Lowlands" at the top. Using information from this chapter and your notes, fill in every area of the organizer. Put it in your notebook.

2. Identify vocabulary from this chapter to add to the vocabulary section of your notebook. Draw diagrams or sketches to help you remember the words and their meanings.

3. Design a coin to illustrate and represent the importance of animal life in the Hudson Bay Lowlands.

## Developing Inquiry/Research and Communication Skills

4. Research an animal found in the Hudson Bay Lowlands. Follow the research model on page 14. Create a mobile that shows each of the following:
   a) title for the mobile
   b) picture of the animal, bird or sea life
   c) where they live
   d) what they eat
   e) why they might be in danger

## Developing Map/Globe Skills

5. Use the map on page 62 to identify hydroelectric development projects that affect the region. Locate and label the hydroelectric power plants and the major rivers on an outline map of the region.

## Applying Concepts and Skills in Various Contexts

6. In groups of three, create a script for a radio or TV commercial promoting the protection of Canada's wetlands. Share your work with one other group.

## Internet Connection

7. Go to www.ontarioparks.com/pola.html to learn more about Polar Bear Provincial Park. You can also go to www.parkscanada.pch.gc.ca/parks/manitoba/wapusk to learn more about Wapusk National Park.

## The Canada Project

1. Find the outline map of Canada you started at the end of Chapter 2. Colour the Hudson Bay Lowlands region. Label the provinces/territories that are in the region. Add important information about the Hudson Bay Lowlands region to your map. (Use the maps on page 62 and inside the front and back covers of the text to help.)

2. Create a tourism brochure for your province/territory that focuses on something special relating to the natural environment. Put it in your scrapbook or shoebox.

# Chapter 7
# The St. Lawrence Lowlands

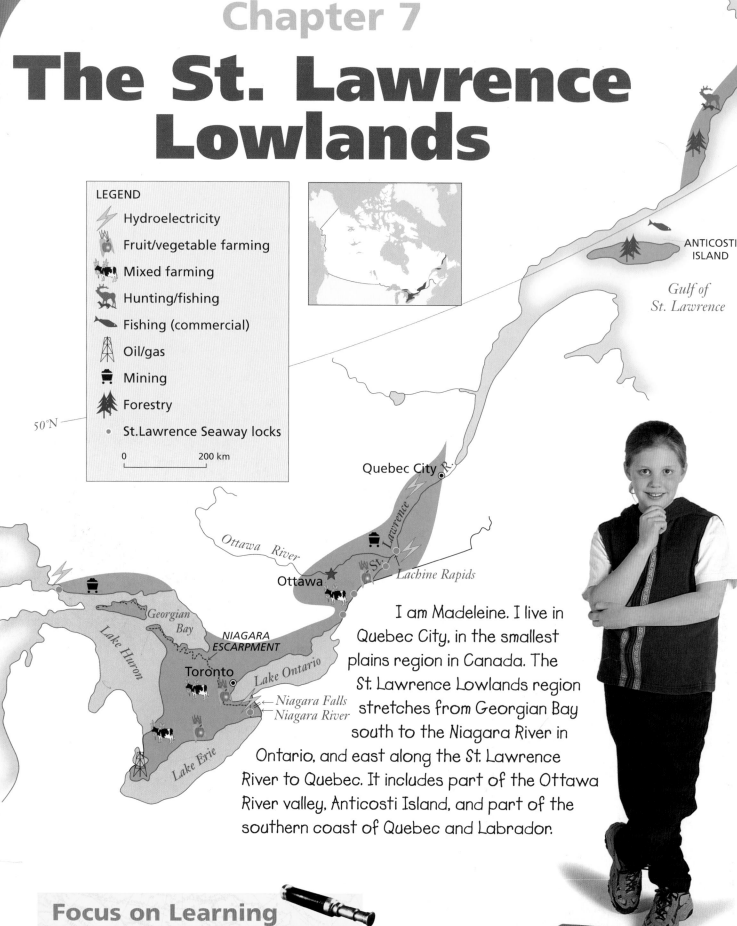

LEGEND

⚡ Hydroelectricity

🍎 Fruit/vegetable farming

🐄 Mixed farming

🦌 Hunting/fishing

🐟 Fishing (commercial)

🗼 Oil/gas

⛏ Mining

🌲 Forestry

• St.Lawrence Seaway locks

0 ——— 200 km

50°N

ANTICOSTI ISLAND

*Gulf of St. Lawrence*

Quebec City

*Ottawa River*

*St. Lawrence R.*

Ottawa

*Lachine Rapids*

*Georgian Bay*

*Lake Huron*

NIAGARA ESCARPMENT

Toronto

*Lake Ontario*

Niagara Falls
Niagara River

*Lake Erie*

I am Madeleine. I live in Quebec City, in the smallest plains region in Canada. The St. Lawrence Lowlands region stretches from Georgian Bay south to the Niagara River in Ontario, and east along the St. Lawrence River to Quebec. It includes part of the Ottawa River valley, Anticosti Island, and part of the southern coast of Quebec and Labrador.

## Focus on Learning

In this chapter you will learn about
- the physical environment of the St. Lawrence Lowlands region
- the Niagara Escarpment
- the St. Lawrence Seaway and locks
- identifying concerns

## Vocabulary

escarpment    sedimentary
estuary       canal
tides         locks

# Physical Features

The St. Lawrence Lowlands region is made up of plains and some hills. The rivers in the region drain into the five Great Lakes and the St. Lawrence River. Particles of earth called sediment are carried by rivers and streams. They have formed a plain with deep, fertile soils.

The region is much lower than the surrounding areas. In parts of the region, the way up to higher ground is very steep. It's like a long rock cliff. This is called an **escarpment**. An escarpment is a barrier to travel. A road, railroad or boat has to make its way up a steep incline to continue onto the higher land.

The St. Lawrence River flows into the Gulf of St. Lawrence through an **estuary**. This is where the mouth of a large river flows into the ocean. Salt water from the ocean mingles with the fresh water of a river.

The water level in the estuary and Gulf of St. Lawrence east of Quebec City is raised and lowered twice a day by tides.

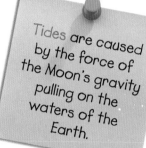

The fertile soils of the plain are good for farming.

Tides are caused by the force of the Moon's gravity pulling on the waters of the Earth.

The plains area along the St. Lawrence River is narrow in some places.

### The Niagara Escarpment

The part of the Niagara Escarpment that is in Ontario is 725 km long. It runs from Queenston on the Niagara River to Manitoulin Island in Georgian Bay. In the highest place, it is 335 metres high. The Niagara River flows over the escarpment at Niagara Falls.

### Do ◆ Discuss ◆ Discover

1. How might people 200 years ago have dealt with travelling up and down an escarpment?
2. Predict what crops might be grown in this region of fertile soil. (You'll find out for sure later in the chapter!)

## Niagara: A Natural Wonder

Did you know that Niagara Falls has moved? When the falls were formed at the end of the last Ice Age, they were 11 km farther downstream!

Water pours off the falls at a rate of 14 million litres per minute. Water rushing over the Horseshoe Falls has broken away the rocks under the falls a little at a time. Erosion changes the position of Niagara Falls 1.2 metres a year.

Niagara Falls is made of three layers of different rocks: dolomite, shale and limestone. The top layer is dolomite. It is a hard, thick layer of **sedimentary** rock. The shale and limestone layers underneath are softer sedimentary rocks. Sedimentary rocks are formed when many layers of particles carried by water have settled on each other and hardened into rock.

The water of the falls flows over the top and lands in the river far below. It splashes back over the face of the falls. Slowly, bits of the softer rock wear away. The dolomite layer on top is undercut. Eventually, another piece of the top layer breaks off and falls into the river. The shape and position of the falls change again.

Niagara Falls is not the highest waterfall in the world, but the greatest volume of water pours over it.

### Do ◆ Discuss ◆ Discover

1. In groups of three, plan an experiment that you could do to demonstrate how the position of the Niagara Falls changes. What materials would you need? What steps would you follow? Are there any special concerns about safety or getting permission for the demonstration? What are they? You do not have to carry out the experiment.

# St. Lawrence Seaway

The St. Lawrence River has been a major water route since earliest times. Aboriginal people, European explorers and settlers all travelled on it.

Large boats could not go farther upstream than the Lachine Rapids in Quebec until the first canal was built.

**Canals** were built to straighten and deepen the river's channel. Then larger boats could pass through. Later, **locks** were built to raise and lower boats in places where elevation changed greatly. Different parts of the waterway were improved at different times.

Since 1959, ships have been able to travel 3790 km inland to Thunder Bay on the west side of Lake Superior.

Lake Superior is the second largest freshwater lake in the world.

Boat traffic on the Seaway today includes everything from huge tankers and cargo ships to tiny pleasure boats.

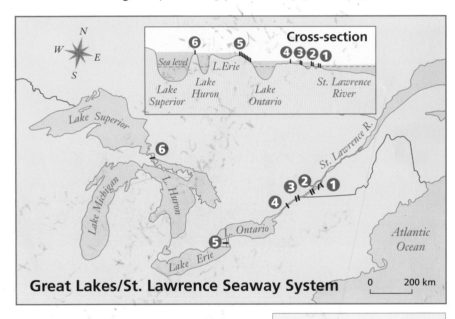

**Great Lakes/St. Lawrence Seaway System**

Cross-section

LEGEND
**Seaway Locks**
1. St. Lambert and Côte Ste. Catherine
2. Beauharnois (2)
3. Snell and Eisenhower
4. Iroquois
5. Welland Canal (8)
6. Sault Ste. Marie

### Do ◆ Discuss ◆ Discover

Work with a partner to research the history of the St. Lawrence Seaway.

1. a) Who used the waterway first?
   b) When were the first canals or locks built?
   c) When were the last built?
2. Create a timeline in the form of a river to display the dates in sequence.

The Seaway looks like a water highway crossing the countryside.

## Locks

A ship is waiting in the Beauharnois lock near Montreal.

> Locks help boats go both upstream and downstream.

There are locks on several sections of the St. Lawrence Seaway. Locks work like an elevator. Watertight "rooms" with gates let ships in at one level. Then the water level changes so they can exit at a different level. The following example shows a boat travelling downstream through a set of locks.

### Step 1

The boat approaches the lock. The gates at both ends of the lock are closed and water is allowed to flow into it. The water level rises to match the river.

### Step 2

The first gate opens and the boat enters the lock. Then the gate closes again.

### Step 3

When both gates are closed, water is released downstream to the river. The level of water in the lock is made equal to the river below.

### Step 4

The downstream gate is opened and the boat travels out of the lock into the river. The gate closes again.

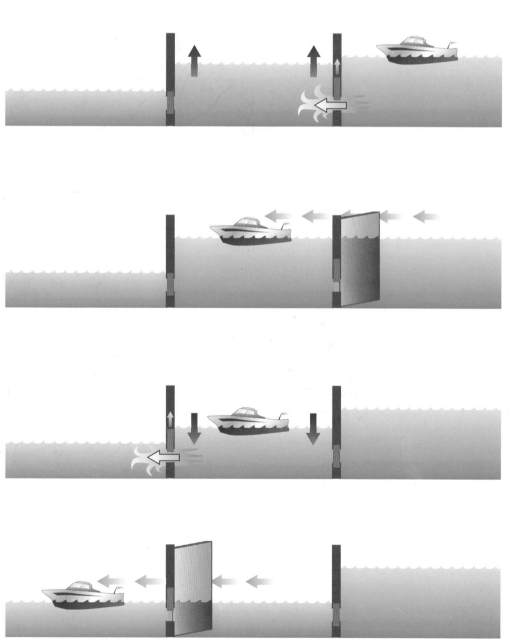

# Climate

This region has hot temperatures and humid weather during the summer. It has one of the longest growing seasons in Canada. The winters are cool and often snowy.

Beaches attract visitors on hot summer days.

The St. Lawrence Lowlands region has several parts. The part closer to the Atlantic Ocean is colder than the part near the Great Lakes. It is farther north. Storms from the Atlantic Ocean are also more frequent there.

The place farthest south in Canada is Middle Island near Point Pelee in Lake Erie. It is at 42° N latitude. The southern border of most of Canada is at the 49th parallel, or 49° N.

Precipitation can come as heavy snowfall in some parts of the region.

# Vegetation

The St. Lawrence Lowlands have old and new forests. The forests contain many kinds of deciduous and coniferous trees. Trees grow to be large because there is plenty of moisture and heat in summer.

Deciduous trees such as birch, maple and walnut grow there. Coniferous trees such as pines, spruce and fir are also present. Many shrubs, flowers and grasses grow abundantly.

The provincial flower of Ontario is the trillium. It blooms in forests throughout the region in early spring.

# Animal Life

Many types of animals live in the St. Lawrence Lowlands region. Land animals include white-tailed deer, squirrels, coyotes, moose, wolves, snowshoe hares and lynx. Warblers, red-winged blackbirds and bluebirds are a few of the many species of birds that make their homes in this region. Many migrating species spend a short time in the region on their way to their summer and winter homes.

This woodpecker has made a nest in a poplar tree.

# Natural Resources

The two most important natural resources of the St. Lawrence Lowlands are the good farming land and the waterway system. This narrow area of plains has fertile soil, a mild climate and plenty of water. Many kinds of fruits and vegetables are grown there. Peaches, apples and grapes are only a few well-known products.

The Great Lakes and the St. Lawrence River form a waterway system over half of the width of Canada! The waterway has been used for transporting goods and people for thousands of years.

Huge ocean-going container ships pass farming communities along the St. Lawrence River.

Apple orchards need many frost-free days to produce ripe fruit for sale.

Dairy farming is an important industry in the region.

The St. Lawrence Lowlands region in Ontario and Quebec contains a huge number of manufacturing industries. They produce countless products. They use natural resources from many different regions, so transportation is important.

Many Canadians benefit from the huge supplies of fresh water in the St. Lawrence Lowlands. Water is used for drinking, cleaning, manufacturing, recreation, agriculture, transportation and creating hydroelectricity.

## Do ◆ Discuss ◆ Discover

1. What kinds of farming and farm products come from the St. Lawrence Lowlands? Remember to think about the different parts of the region. List five different types in your notebook.

2. List the different uses and benefits of the St. Lawrence Seaway system. Identify how many of these affect you personally. Briefly describe how.

## St. Lawrence Lowlands Arts

Quilts are a fabric art. They are made of many pieces of cloth sewed together to form a pattern. Many quilts show an abstract pattern. Others present a picture made of many colours and textures of cloth.

Patterns may use the same pieces repeated in different ways, or different pieces repeated in a regular way. Contrast is important.

The Road Not Taken, created by Bridget O'Flaherty, Perth, ON

## Patterns

Dark and light and dark
Ripple and echo
Like two tom-toms and a flute
Calling across the far lake water.
And moonlight shines on the boat dock
Of your last summer cottage night.

Tomorrow you will drive
And drive through miles
   of forest, fireweed, smoke stacks, rail cars,
   gravel pits, side roads, dusty school buses,
And fast food outlets.

To the familiar streets of home
The familiar ring of the telephone
The washing machine groaning lowly
And your own bed back at last.

– B. Gibbs

Envelopes, created by Bridget O'Flaherty, Perth, ON

### Do ◆ Discuss ◆ Discover

1. Discuss with a partner how the image in the quilt *The Road Not Taken* represents the St. Lawrence Lowlands.

2. Create a work of art based on pattern. You can choose to use sounds, colours, textures or images to make your pattern.

# Madeleine's Concern

My aunt plans educational trips of the waterways of this region. For example, she guides boat tours to see the whales in the Gulf of St. Lawrence.

Many industries are located near the St. Lawrence River system. Factories and industries are a source of water and air pollution. Sometimes, smoke is heavy and dark in this area.

The population of the St. Lawrence Lowlands is very high. There are more people per square kilometre than in any other region of Canada. Automobiles, homes and businesses all produce smoke and wastes.

The people in this region are concerned about the pollution levels. During some summers, some beaches are too polluted for swimming. Acid rain from air pollution kills vegetation and affects building materials. Fish are sometimes found dead on shorelines.

Everybody needs to help in order to make a difference. I am concerned that as the population continues to grow, these problems will increase. We need to plan for the future to prevent this.

WARNING
POLLUTED WATERS
PERSONS BATHING
DO SO AT THEIR OWN RISK

### Do ◆ Discuss ◆ Discover

1. Discuss possible reasons for this region having so many people and industries.
2. Discuss the many uses of the waterway and the effects that large numbers of people and industries have on it.

# Chapter 7

## Understanding Concepts

1. Draw a region organizer similar to the one you did on page 69 of Chapter 6. Write the title "The St. Lawrence Lowlands" at the top. Using information from this chapter and your notes, fill in every area of the organizer. Put it in your notebook.

2. Identify vocabulary from this chapter to add to the vocabulary section of your notebook. Draw diagrams or sketches to help you remember the words and their meanings.

3. Draw your own diagram of how a lock works. Include an explanation in your own words.

## Developing Inquiry/Research and Communication Skills

4. Keep a one-day journal of the ways water is used around your home. Research how you can reduce the use of water in your home. (Follow the research model on page 14.) Discuss your findings with two other students in your class.

5. Research Niagara Falls. Create a one-page magazine advertisement with pictures and information of the different places and activities in Niagara Falls.

## Developing Map/Globe Skills

6. Sketch or trace the St. Lawrence Seaway diagram on page 73. Label all the parts and put it in your notebook.

7. On an outline map of the region, locate and label major cities along the St. Lawrence Seaway. Also identify and label the major transportation routes in this region. Include ship, air, road and railroad routes.

## Applying Concepts and Skills in Various Contexts

8. Create a flyer advertising a Clean-Up-the-Beach Day for a community. Remember to include date, time and anything special that people need to bring or wear.

## The Canada Project

1. Find the outline map of Canada you started at the end of Chapter 2. Colour the St. Lawrence Lowlands region and label the provinces/territories in the region. Add important information about the St. Lawrence Lowlands region to your map. (Use the maps on page 70 and inside the front and back covers of the text to help.)

2. On an outline map of your province/territory, locate and label all major rivers, lakes and bodies of water. On the back of the map or a separate piece of paper, create a chart listing the major waterways and the uses and benefits of each. Put it in your scrapbook or shoebox.

# Chapter 8
# The Appalachian Region

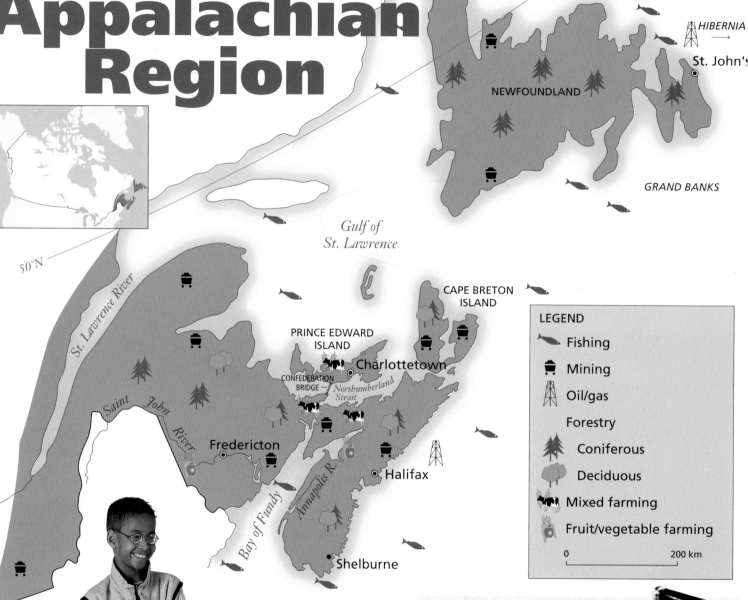

HIBERNIA →

St. John's

NEWFOUNDLAND

GRAND BANKS

50°N

Gulf of
St. Lawrence

St. Lawrence River

CAPE BRETON
ISLAND

PRINCE EDWARD
ISLAND

Charlottetown

CONFEDERATION
BRIDGE — Northumberland
Strait

Saint John River

Fredericton

Halifax

Bay of Fundy

Annapolis R.

Shelburne

LEGEND

🐟 Fishing

⛏ Mining

🛢 Oil/gas

Forestry
🌲 Coniferous
🌳 Deciduous

🐄 Mixed farming

Fruit/vegetable farming

0          200 km

My name is Lincoln, and I come from the Appalachian region. Several provinces of Canada lie completely within the region: New Brunswick, Nova Scotia and Prince Edward Island. Parts of Quebec and the island of Newfoundland are also part of the Appalachian region.

## Focus on Learning

In this chapter you will learn about
- the physical environment of the Appalachian region
- how tides work
- the Confederation Bridge
- a fishing community
- identifying concerns

## Vocabulary

| | |
|---|---|
| ocean current | harvest |
| continental shelf | inshore fishing |
| Grand Banks | trawler |
| tidal range | offshore fishing |
| gale | aquaculture |

# Physical Features

The Appalachian region is part of a low range of mountains. Scientists call these mountains "old." They were created long before the mountains of the Cordillera. They have been worn down by erosion over millions of years.

Rocky cliffs, islands, bays, protected harbours and beaches are found along the coast.

The region faces the Atlantic Ocean. It has thousands of kilometres of sea coast. The bigger islands within this region are Prince Edward Island, Newfoundland and Cape Breton Island. Waves, ocean currents and tides erode the cliffs and form beaches in the region.

An ocean current is a stream of moving water within a larger body of water. A drifting boat caught in an ocean current can be carried many kilometres along a coast or out to sea.

Off the shores of the Appalachian region, the ocean floor slants downward gradually. Then it drops off abruptly into a deep trench. The slanting ocean floor is called the **continental shelf**. Southeast of Newfoundland lie several shallower parts of the continental shelf. They are called the **Grand Banks**, and they are famous as a fishing ground.

The plains and valley areas of the region have fertile soils in some places. In other places they are rocky or boggy.

People who swim or fish in the ocean must learn about the tides and ocean currents in order to be safe.

A green valley along the St. John River in New Brunswick

## Do ◆ Discuss ◆ Discover

1. In a small group, create a pamphlet about the tides and the ocean currents to alert tourists who are visiting the beaches of the Appalachian region.

### Tides

Tides are changes in the level of the water caused by the pull of the moon's gravity.

The water rises for about six hours, as it flows towards the shore. Then

At low tide, these boats along the Bay of Fundy rest on the bottom. As the water rises, they will float again.

the water begins to flow back out to sea again. This also lasts about six hours. The difference between the water level at high tide and at low tide is called the tidal range.

Tides move the waters of the Earth. They bring fresh food and oxygen to plants and animals living near shore, and they take away waste products. The tides in the Annapolis, Nova Scotia, area power a generating station that creates electricity for the area.

*The Bay of Fundy has the highest tides in the world. The difference between high and low tide can be as much as 15 metres. Compare this to the height of your house roof!*

# Climate

Plentiful rainfall helps forests to grow.

The climate in the Appalachian region varies. The summers may be cool or warm and rainy. The long winters have much precipitation. Precipitation ranges from about 1100 mm to 1400 mm per year.

The Northumberland Strait between Prince Edward Island and the mainland freezes in the winter. Fierce storms called gales are common in winter. Winter wind speeds may reach 100 km per hour on the islands and shoreline.

*Winds over 50 to 60 km per hour are considered to be gale force winds.*

Ice storms and snowstorms are frequent on the Atlantic coast.

### Do ◆ Discuss ◆ Discover

1. Do an Internet search to learn more about gales and the Northumberland Strait. In a small group, create a weather report warning travellers of a fierce storm coming the next day. Read your report out loud to another group.

# The Confederation Bridge

The Confederation Bridge was built to connect Prince Edward Island and New Brunswick. It was officially opened on May 31, 1997. The bridge is 12.9 kilometres long.

The Confederation Bridge was designed to withstand the severe weather in the Northumberland Strait. For many years engineers studied the effects that the tides, gales and sea ice would have on the structure. For example, they designed the bridge supports to split apart ice floes that hit them as they move through the Strait.

A weather station monitors weather conditions on the bridge 24 hours a day. It reports wind speed, wind direction, air temperature, road temperature, humidity and precipitation.

When the weather is bad, the bridge is closed to traffic. People must then take the ferry to Prince Edward Island, just as they did before the bridge was completed.

The Confederation Bridge is the longest bridge ever built over ice-covered water.

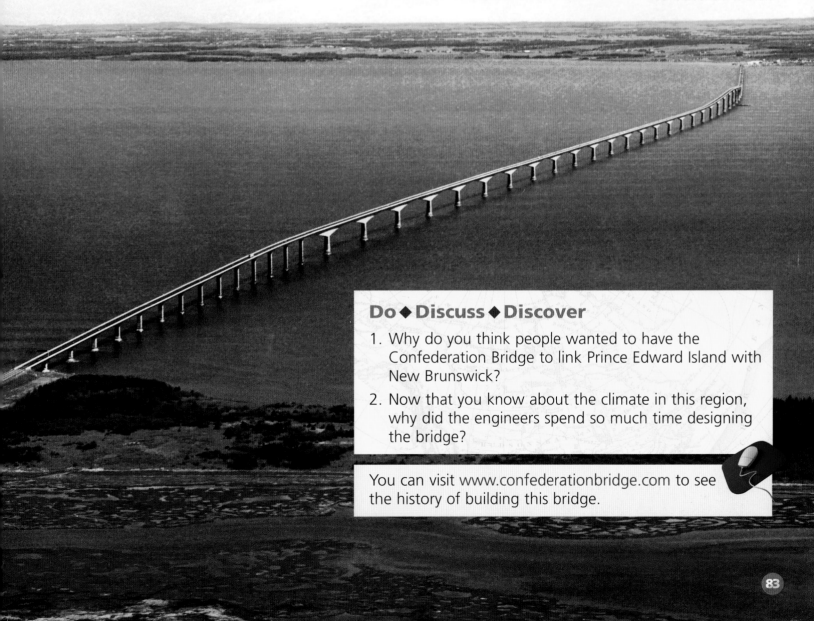

## Do ◆ Discuss ◆ Discover

1. Why do you think people wanted to have the Confederation Bridge to link Prince Edward Island with New Brunswick?

2. Now that you know about the climate in this region, why did the engineers spend so much time designing the bridge?

You can visit www.confederationbridge.com to see the history of building this bridge.

# Vegetation

Mixed forests of oak, red maple, spruce and white pine grow in valleys and lower areas.

Much of the mainland Appalachian region is forested. Coniferous trees grow in the higher areas, both inland and on the coast. Forests of black and white spruce and balsam fir are found there. Hardwood forests of white and yellow birch, beech and sugar maple once grew in the higher areas. They have been almost completely logged.

Trees grow slowly in the Appalachian region. The climate is often harsh. The soil is rocky or not fertile in many places.

Whales are found in the Gulf of St. Lawrence, but they have been affected by polluted waters.

# Animal Life

In the past, this area has been one of the richest ocean fishing grounds in the world. Cod fish used to be very plentiful. Today smaller numbers of fish are found in this area.

Grey seals and harbour seals can be found in estuaries and harbours.

The mainland Appalachian region is home to many different species of animals. Mammals include white-tailed deer, fox, snowshoe hare, coyote, mink, otter, muskrat, porcupine, beaver and raccoon.

The island of Newfoundland once had fewer types of land animals than other parts of the region. Many have been introduced there, including moose, caribou, snowshoe hare and squirrel.

Great blue herons and many species of ducks, shorebirds and waterfowl can be found along the beaches and in marshes and lagoons.

Bonaventure Island is a migratory bird sanctuary. It is home to puffins, gulls and razorbills.

Thousands of seabirds, such as puffins, gulls, and auks breed on rocky cliffs and islands.

## Do ◆ Discuss ◆ Discover

1. a) Choose one animal from this region to research.
   b) Write a postcard fact sheet on the animal. Place important information about the animal on one side and include a picture on the other.
   c) Write four Who Am I clues for the animal.
   d) With a partner, play the Who Am I game and then share your postcard with them.

# Natural Resources

In the past, the Appalachian region has been known for its coal mines and its fishing. Many of the coal mines of the region are now closed, as the costs to operate them became greater. The fishing industry has also become weaker as ocean fish become fewer.

Some zinc and lead, potash, salt, asbestos, copper and gold are mined in the region. There are also two offshore oil fields. One is on the continental shelf near Nova Scotia. The other is on the Grand Banks near Newfoundland.

The oil field on the Grand Banks is called Hibernia.

## Fishing

Cod, salmon, pollock, halibut, redfish, herring, swordfish, sole, flounder, haddock, clams, oysters, scallops and lobster are all harvested in the Atlantic region. The government makes laws to help conserve the fish stocks.

The government prevents other countries from fishing closer than 200 nautical miles from Canada's shore. (A nautical mile is about 1850 metres.) It does this to protect this valuable resource.

There are two types of commercial fishing. One is **inshore fishing**. Small boats, used mainly by families, harvest cod and lobster for local restaurants and tourist areas. They operate from May to September.

The word harvest is often used to describe the collecting stage of certain industries. Farming, fishing and lumbering are three examples.

Large fishing boats, or **trawlers**, go out into the ocean in fleets to catch the fish. This is **offshore fishing**. They drag steel mesh nets along the ocean floor to scoop up fish. Large fishing boats can clean and process the fish at sea. They can operate year round.

The government controls the number of fish that can be caught so that the fishing industry will continue to provide food and jobs for Canadians.

## Do ◆ Discuss ◆ Discover

1. Why would the government protect the fishing industry by preventing other countries from fishing inside the 200 nautical mile limit?

# A Fishing Community

I live in Shelburne, Nova Scotia. This community was founded in the southwest corner of the province in the 1780s. It has a population of 2245. Its natural harbour is considered the third-best in the world.

Shelburne began as a fishing and shipbuilding centre. Many historic buildings still exist. Tourists come to see what an Atlantic fishing town looked like in the past.

Fishing is still very important. However, today we are involved in a new industry called aquaculture. Aquaculture combines fishing and farming, because fish are raised like a crop. Read the following article about aquaculture that was in my school newspaper.

## A new fish story

For the last few years, fishermen have been discouraged by the news that our ocean fish stocks are being slowly used up. The government wanted us to lower the number of fish we caught on the Grand Banks and off the coast of our province. But all over the country, people are demanding fish as a source of food. We have to find new ways to provide fish.

What is aquaculture? It is fish farming. The workers create a series of containers, similar to large pools. These containers hold the fish at the different stages of their development.

*Aquaculture ponds at a fish farm*

Aquaculture, just like farming, involves seeding, feeding and harvesting of fish. Fish eggs are hatched, the fish are fed, and when they are full grown they are harvested. Fish have been farmed in other parts of the world for many centuries. However, it is a new industry here—only 25 years old. Fish farmers here are raising blue mussels, European oysters, steelhead salmon and sea scallops.

Many people are excited about aquaculture. It is like farming the sea, and it's an alternative to fishing. The opportunities for selling fish to other countries are excellent. Aquaculture should also provide many jobs in future.

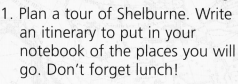

## Visit Shelburne

1. Plan a tour of Shelburne. Write an itinerary to put in your notebook of the places you will go. Don't forget lunch!

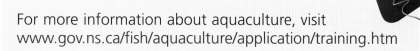

For more information about aquaculture, visit www.gov.ns.ca/fish/aquaculture/application/training.htm

# The Newfoundland Cod

Basking in the sun
One summer day
Was a giant cod
At Fortune Bay.
I stepped on this cod
In Newfoundland,
Stepped on its head
As it slept on the sand.

It sprang to its tail
By the sunny sea.
It bugged its eyes
And screamed at me:
"Kiss me or tickle me,
Hug me or pickle me,
Jiggle me, wiggle me,
Suddenly squiggle me.
Take me and flake me,
Shake me and bake me.
Batter me, fry me,
Poach me or dry me.
But keep your stinking
Feet away
From codfish sunning
At Fortune Bay!"

As it wiggled its way
Back into the sea
A monster wave
Washed over me.
It spanked me
With a dozen whacks
From Newfoundland
To Halifax.

And…
Never, ever
Since that day
Have I stepped on a cod
At Fortune Bay.

– Robert Heidbreder

## Do ◆ Discuss ◆ Discover

Read the poem on this page and discuss the following questions.

1. a) Why might this be called a "nonsense poem"?

   b) Give examples of the way the author uses sounds to create a certain effect in the poem.

   c) Give examples of images the author uses to help you "see" the scene.

# Lincoln's Concern

My mom is a marine biologist. We live in Shelburne. When she comes home at night, we like to talk. Often we discuss how her day went and the things I have learned in school. The other day we discussed the way the numbers of fish have declined. It is very difficult for people to make a living fishing.

My mom had lots of information about why the fish stocks were getting so low. She explained that trawlers catch both young and adult fish. If younger fish are not left to become adults, hatchings of new fish will not be born.

Regulations have become stricter. However, some kinds of fish and shellfish will take a long time to increase their numbers. This problem affects everyone in my town.

The young people in my community are concerned about the future of the fishing industry and the fish in the Atlantic Ocean.

Many large fishing companies take fish out of the same area. Trawlers come from a number of different countries to compete with Canadian companies for fish in the ocean.

## Do ◆ Discuss ◆ Discover

1. Discuss reasons that explain the declining numbers of fish. (Use the information from above and earlier in the chapter.)
2. Discuss the different ways lower numbers of fish could affect a community such as Shelburne.

# Chapter 8

## Understanding Concepts

1. Draw a region organizer similar to the one you did on page 79 of Chapter 7. Write the title "The Appalachian" at the top. Use information from this chapter and your notes to fill in every area of the organizer. Put it in your notebook.

2. Identify vocabulary from this chapter to add to the vocabulary section of your notebook. Draw diagrams or sketches to help you remember the words and their meanings.

3. Create a web about the Grand Banks and put it in your notebook.

## Developing Inquiry/Research and Communication Skills

4. Research the different methods used by inshore and offshore fishing vessels to catch fish. Follow the research model on page 14. Draw and label a picture of each method.

## Applying Concepts and Skills in Various Contexts

5. Listen to some traffic reports on the radio. Write the script for a traffic report for the Confederation Bridge on a windy winter day. Record or read aloud your traffic report for your classmates.

## Internet Connection

6. Visit the Confederation Bridge website at www.confederationbridge.com. Work in a small group to create a fact card (like a baseball card) for the bridge statistics. Include facts such as how long it is and how many people travel on it. Remember to include a picture of the bridge on the front.

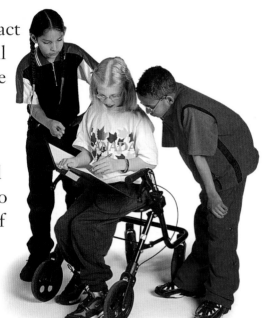

## The Canada Project

1. Find the outline map of Canada you started at the end of Chapter 2. Colour the Appalachian region. Label the provinces/territories in the region. Add important information about the Appalachian region to your map. (Use the maps on page 80 and inside the front and back covers of the text to help.)

2. Identify a natural land formation created by water or wind in your province/territory. Find a picture or draw your own illustration of the landform. On the back, write a short paragraph explaining how the landform was created. Put it in your scrapbook or shoebox.

3. Put all the organizers you have filled in for regions that are in your province or territory into your scrapbook or shoebox.

# Chapter 9
# Our Provinces and Territories

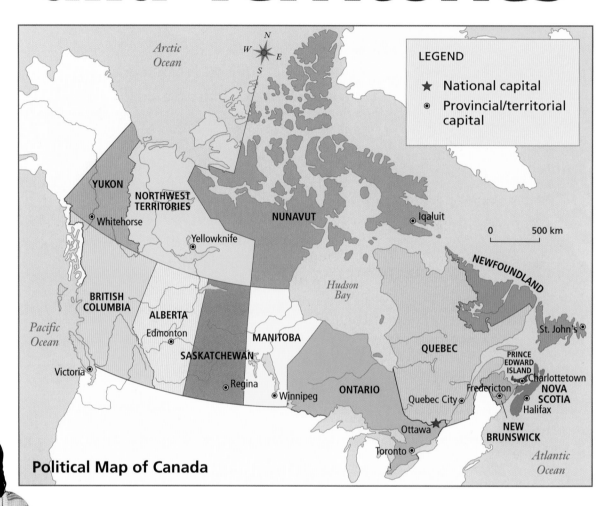

**Political Map of Canada**

Arctic Ocean

LEGEND
★ National capital
⊙ Provincial/territorial capital

YUKON
NORTHWEST TERRITORIES
⊙ Whitehorse
NUNAVUT
⊙ Iqaluit
⊙ Yellowknife
0    500 km
NEWFOUNDLAND
Hudson Bay
BRITISH COLUMBIA
ALBERTA
Pacific Ocean
⊙ Edmonton
MANITOBA
SASKATCHEWAN
St. John's ⊙
⊙ Victoria
QUEBEC
PRINCE EDWARD ISLAND
⊙ Regina
⊙ Winnipeg
ONTARIO
Fredericton ⊙ Charlottetown
NOVA SCOTIA
Quebec City ⊙
Halifax
Ottawa ★
NEW BRUNSWICK
Toronto ⊙
Atlantic Ocean

We have been looking at our country, Canada, in different ways. We have looked at the seven physical regions and at our rich natural resources.

The map on this page shows Canada's political divisions. Canada is divided into ten provinces and three territories. Each has a capital city, where its government meets.

## Focus on Learning

In this chapter you will learn about
• locating and labeling the different provinces, territories and capital cities
• Ottawa, the capital of Canada
• map reading using a grid
• characteristics of each province and territory
• boundaries on maps

## Vocabulary

| | |
|---|---|
| province | grid |
| territory | boundary |
| capital city | border |
| federal government | municipal |
| longitude | |

# Describing Political Regions

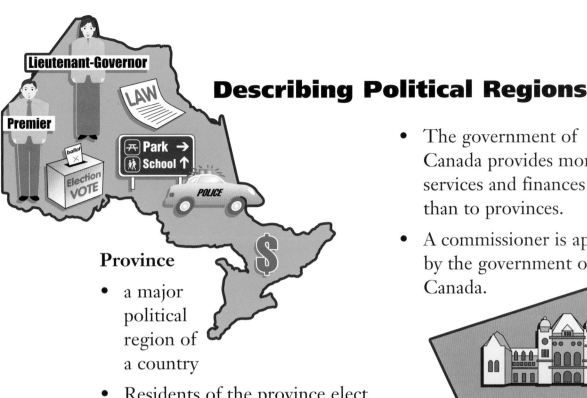

*Coming Up*
You will learn more about government in Chapter 10.

## Province

- a major political region of a country

- Residents of the province elect the provincial government.

- The provincial government makes many laws and provides many services.

- Residents pay for the government and services through taxes.

- The government of Canada provides some services and finances.

## Territory

- a political region that is not yet a province. It usually has a small population in a large area.

- Residents of the territory elect the territorial government.

- The territorial government makes some laws and provides some services.

- Residents pay for the government and some services through taxes.

- The government of Canada provides more services and finances than to provinces.

- A commissioner is appointed by the government of Canada.

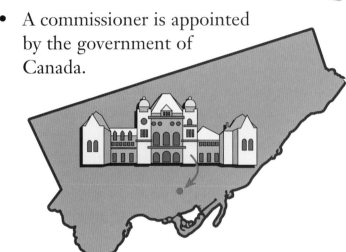

## Capital city

- a city in a country, province or territory containing the government buildings

- not always the largest city in a country, province or territory

- The national capital of Canada is Ottawa, Ontario.

- The provincial capital of Ontario is Toronto.

### Do ◆ Discuss ◆ Discover

1. Add the three terms on this page to the vocabulary section of your notebook.

2. Find the outline map of Canada from Chapter 1 on which you labelled the provinces and territories and the places from which the seven children came. Now add the capital cities of each province and territory and Ottawa to this map.

3. Playing games will help you learn the names of the provinces and territories and their capital cities. Invent a simple game with a partner and play it with them. Exchange games with another pair of students.

# Our National Capital

Ottawa is the capital of Canada. The federal government meets there. It deals with concerns and makes laws that affect the whole country. Members of the federal government are known as Members of Parliament, or MPs.

Thousands of people come to the Parliament Buildings in Ottawa to celebrate Canada Day.

The Byward Market is one of the oldest parts of Ottawa. It is famous for shopping and entertainment.

The National Gallery of Canada has a wonderful collection of art. There are many museums in Ottawa.

## Do ◆ Discuss ◆ Discover

1. Draw a four-season picture of how the Rideau Canal can be used for fun and recreation year round.

2. On a page in your notebook, create a web of reasons to visit Ottawa. Leave room to add more reasons as you read further in this chapter.

The Rideau Canal is used for skating in the winter and boating in the summer.

# Map Reading: Grids

Look carefully at the globe. Notice the set of lines that runs east–west, parallel to the Equator. These are called lines of latitude.

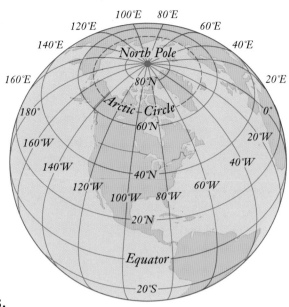

A second set of lines runs north–south. These lines are not parallel. They are farthest apart at the Equator and meet at the North Pole and the South Pole. These are called lines of **longitude**.

Places on Earth can be named or described using their latitude and longitude position. The two sets of lines form a **grid**. A grid divides an area up into blocks.

Maps provide grids to help you locate places on them. A grid is like a table made up of columns and rows. The columns are identified with alphabet letters and the rows identified with numbers. The numbers and letters on the grid help you name the blocks. This is a sample of a grid.

To find an item on a grid, put a finger of your right hand on the correct letter block. Put a finger of your left hand on the correct number block. Slide your right finger down the column. At the same time, slide the left finger across the row. Where the two fingers meet is the item on the grid.

## Do ◆ Discuss ◆ Discover

1. What symbol is in block A2? What symbol is in block C3?
2. Make a grid, adding your own symbols or pictures. Make up five questions about items on your grid. Work with a partner to practise finding symbols on each other's grids.

# Touring Ottawa

Today we are going to tour the city of Ottawa. All the sights of the city are close together and easy to find. We will work in teams to follow the scavenger hunt clues on the next page. Follow the map, and visit some of the sites of Ottawa.

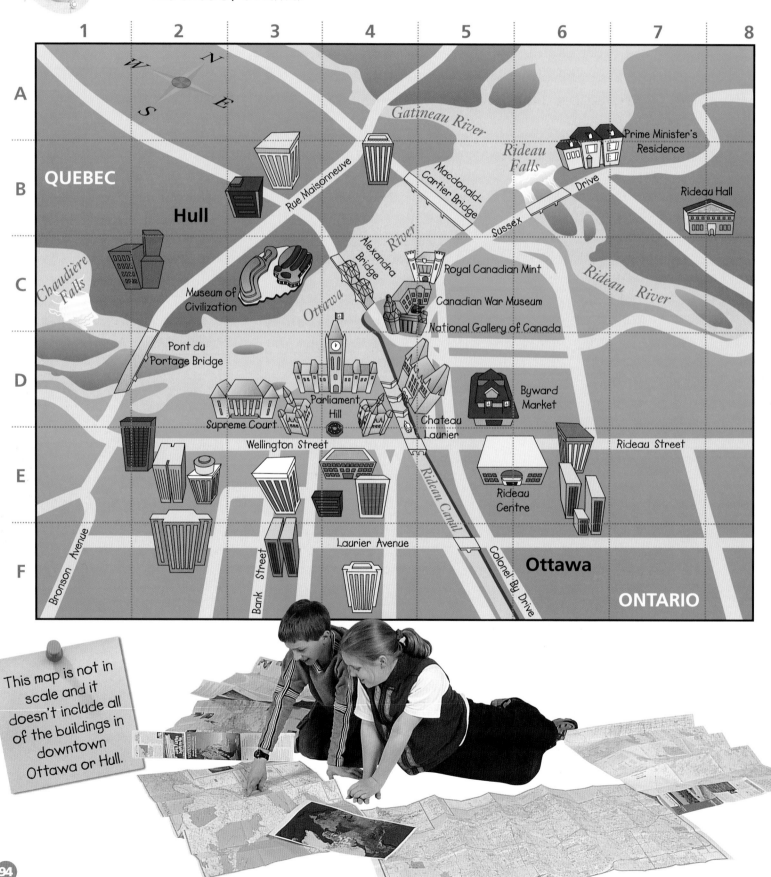

This map is not in scale and it doesn't include all of the buildings in downtown Ottawa or Hull.

## Tour Instructions

1. Leave the Chateau Laurier hotel (D5) and turn west on Wellington Street. As you cross the bridge, look north. On what canal is this set of locks?

2. Walk west to Parliament Hill. It is in grid square D4. The Flame in front of the Parliament Building was lit in 1967 to celebrate Canada's 100th birthday. How old is Canada today?

3. You can tour the Centre Block on Parliament Hill to visit the Library. This was the only part of the building that survived a fire in 1916. What can you climb to see a view of the city?

4. Go back to Wellington Street and walk to D3. There you can tour Canada's highest court of law. You must be very quiet. The judges are making decisions that will affect all Canadians. What is this building called?

5. Hop on the bus and cross the Pont de Portage. As you cross, look west. What body of water can you see in the background?

6. The bus drops you off in block C3. What city and province are you in now? What is the name of the museum there?

7. Cross the bridge east of the museum. This will bring you back to Ottawa. Go to the building made of steel and glass in C4. You will see many types of visual art. What is the name of this building?

8. In grid square C5 you will find a museum that displays the money used in Canada. What is the name of this museum?

9. Another museum near it displays uniforms and weapons used by soldiers who fought in wars around the world. What is the museum's name?

10. Walk to the market in D5. It is famous for a delicious treat called Beaver Tails. These are pastries shaped like a beaver tail. They are topped with sugar and cinnamon, or just about anything you like!

For more information, visit www.ottawakiosk.com and www.capcan.ca

95

# Learning about Provinces and Territories

Let's share the task of learning about 13 different provinces and territories! This is an opportunity for you to help others learn and have others help you.

Your teacher has already set up groups for working together on provinces and territories. Each group will present information to the rest of the class about one province or territory.

The maps inside the front and back covers of the textbook provide useful information about Canada.

Everyone will be expected to ask questions and discuss each presentation with the group doing it. You will also need to put information about each presentation in your notebook.

Each presenting group will give you a province/territory fact sheet.

The materials that your group makes for this presentation will be part of your final Canada Project. Include all five of the following parts in your presentation.

1. a list of "Fast Facts"
   • name of province/territory
   • capital city
   • land area
   • official symbols
   • population
   • major imports and exports
   • special features such as "the biggest…" or "the tallest…"

2. a description of the physical features, climate, vegetation, animals and natural resources

   • Identify each physical region and explain where it is found in your province/territory.
   • Choose an interesting form for this part: for example, a news report, a booklet or pamphlet, a scroll, a photo essay, a series of drawings with captions.

3. copies of notes to hand out to your audience (summarize the facts in numbers 1 and 2)

4. a map, with boundaries, major landforms and bodies of water, important places, capital city, and natural resources

   • Include all of the correct parts of a map.

5. a creative form showing or telling about something special in your province or territory

   • for example, a poem and picture, a story, a model or sculpture, a painting, a slideshow, a play or a poster

# British Columbia

## Fast Facts

- 930 000 square km of land
- 4 million people
- Cordillera region

Nickname: Beautiful BC

Capital: Victoria

Exports: lumber, pulp (for paper), coal, natural gas, oil, electrical power, minerals, fish and shellfish, vegetables, fruit, berries, flowers, machinery

Imports: manufactured goods, wheat and farm products

## Environment

- rocky islands, high mountains, deep inlets on Pacific coast
- mild and damp climate
- some of world's largest trees in Pacific Rim National Park
- three ranges of mountains, fast rivers, and deep valleys affect transportation routes
- small amount of agricultural land in valleys and on plateaus

## Natural Resources

- salmon, herring, cod, oysters and halibut caught in the ocean and river mouths
- coal, oil and natural gas
- metals include gold, lead, zinc and silver; non-metals include gypsum and gravel
- major hydroelectric dams on the Peace River, Fraser River and Columbia River
- lumber from the forests produces 40% of all manufactured wood in Canada

## Industries and Products

- industries: forestry, wood and paper, mining, tourism, recreation, agriculture, fishing, manufacturing
- grapes, apples, peaches, plums, apricots, pears and cherries grown in Okanagan Valley
- vegetables, berries, fruits, flowers and dairy products from Lower Fraser Valley
- beef cattle raised on grasslands on the interior plateau
- manufacturing mainly based on natural resources

## People and Places

- Vancouver, the largest city, is at the mouth of the Fraser River. It is the third largest city in Canada.
- Victoria, the provincial capital, is on Vancouver Island.

## Something Special

- varied and beautiful environment
- Butchart Gardens in Victoria
- Capilano suspension bridge
- totem poles and West Coast First Nations art

## Websites

For more information about BC, visit www.hellobc.com, www.gov.bc.ca and www.travel.bc.ca

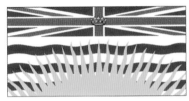

Pacific Dogwood

Steller's Jay

The city of Vancouver is located between the mountains of the Cordillera and the salt water of the Pacific Ocean.

Fireweed

Common Raven

# Yukon Territory

## Fast Facts

- 483 000 square km of land
- 30 600 people
- Cordillera and Arctic Lowlands regions

Nickname: North of 60

Capital: Whitehorse

Exports: minerals, pulp and paper

Imports: manufactured goods, fresh food and dairy products, wheat and farm products, machinery

## Environment

- north of 60° N latitude, partly within the Arctic Circle
- mostly in the Cordillera region; small amount of Arctic Lowlands on the north coast
- mountainous and beautiful
- long cold winters and permafrost
- few roads or people
- several huge glaciers and largest non-polar icefields in the world
- Aurora Borealis (Northern Lights)
- large numbers of animals: wood bison and musk oxen; last remaining large herd of barren ground caribou; moose, mountain sheep, deer, timber wolves, black and brown bears, grizzly bears

- summer breeding grounds of geese, swans, ducks and numerous shorebirds; ptarmigan remain all year
- Arctic grayling, northern pike, rainbow and lake trout, whitefish and salmon

## Natural Resources

- minerals: lead, zinc, gold, silver, copper, coal

## Industries and Products

- most important industries are mining and tourism
- tourism: fishing, river rafting, hiking, camping and canoeing in unspoiled environment

## People and Places

- Whitehorse is the territorial capital of Yukon. It is also the regional headquarters for the Royal Canadian Mounted Police. It is on a major transportation route linking Canada and Alaska. Two-thirds of the population of Yukon Territory lives in Whitehorse.

## Something Special

- Klondike Gold Rush took place over 100 years ago
- hosts Arctic Winter games every 6 years

## Websites

For more information about Yukon Territory, visit www.gov.yk.ca and www.touryukon.com

Mount Logan in Kluane National Park is the highest point in Canada.

# Alberta

## Fast Facts

- 644 000 square km of land
- 3 million people
- Interior Plains and Cordillera regions

Nickname: Sunny Alberta

Capital: Edmonton

Exports: oil and gas, wheat and agricultural products, meat products, wood pulp and paper, machinery

Imports: manufactured goods, seafood products, machinery

## Environment

- wide variety of landforms: mountains, foothills, plains and badlands. Badlands have little precipitation, but in the past, erosion has carved deep gullies and ravines. Many fossils of dinosaurs have been found in the badlands.
- Rocky Mountains and foothills of the Rockies along western border
- Cypress Hills in southeastern Alberta have unique types of vegetation

## Natural Resources

- largest amount of land suitable for farming or ranching of any province or territory
- largest deposits of oil and gas
- coal, forests, hydroelectricity

## Industries and Products

- oil and gas industry most important source of income and employment
- plastics and other products made from oil
- forestry, pulp and paper, tourism

## People and Places

- Edmonton is the provincial capital city. It is a centre for grain shipping and meat processing and has many oil refineries. It is Canada's fifth largest city.
- Calgary, in southern Alberta, has main offices of many oil and gas companies. It is Canada's fourth largest city.
- Calgary hosted the Winter Olympics in 1988.
- Banff, in the Rocky Mountains, was Canada's first National Park. Visitors come to see the natural wonders and many types of wildlife.

## Something Special

- an NHL-size skating rink, a huge pool with its own beach and waves, and performing dolphins at West Edmonton Mall
- chuckwagon races at the Calgary Stampede

## Websites

To learn more about Alberta, visit www.gov.ab.ca, www.discoveralberta.com and www.dinosaurvalley.com

Wild Rose

Great Horned Owl

In the Alberta badlands, hoodoos were formed by erosion where a layer of harder rock sits on top of softer rock.

Mountain Avens

Gyrfalcon

# Northwest Territories

## Fast Facts

- 3.3 million square km of land
- 41 600 people
- Cordillera, Interior Plains, Arctic Lowlands and Canadian Shield regions

Nickname: Land of the Midnight Sun

Capital: Yellowknife

Exports: minerals, oil and gas, works of art, pulp and paper

Imports: fresh foods and dairy products, manufactured goods, machinery

## Environment

- north of 60° N
- huge land of mountains, forests, tundra, clean rivers and thousands of clear lakes
- sun never sets at mid-summer; never rises at mid-winter
- Aurora Borealis (Northern Lights)
- animal life includes white foxes and white whales, several kinds of bears, and herds of bison, moose and caribou

## Natural Resources

- oil and gas reserves under the Beaufort Sea and Mackenzie Delta
- minerals: uranium, copper, gold, lead and zinc
- diamonds mined near Lac de Gras, about 300 km northeast of Yellowknife

## Industries and Products

- oil wells
- gold mining
- fur trapping
- commercial fishing for whitefish, pickerel, Arctic char
- tourism and recreation
- arts and crafts

## People and Places

- a small population in a large land area: communities along the Mackenzie, Liard and Peel Rivers, on large lakes, and along the Arctic coast
- Yellowknife is the capital of the Northwest Territories. It is a centre for business, mining, transportation and government services. The Mackenzie Highway connects Yellowknife with Edmonton, almost 1000 km to the south.

## Something Special

- Many Inuit and First Nations people live traditional lifestyles, gathering their own food from the land. However, modern bungalow homes and snowmobiles are common. Satellite television and the Internet connect many people to the rest of the world.

## Websites

To learn more about the Northwest Territories, visit www.gov.nt.ca and www.nwttravel.nt.ca

Transportation by air is very important in the Northwest Territories.

# Saskatchewan

## Fast Facts

- 570 700 square km of land
- 1 million people
- Interior Plains and Canadian Shield regions

Nickname: The Breadbasket of Canada

Capital: Regina

Exports: cereal grains, oil seeds (e.g., canola), machinery, oil, potash, uranium

Imports: manufactured goods, electricity, seafood products

## Environment

- a vast flat land in the south; the second largest plains area
- huge region of Canadian Shield, with rocks, lakes and forests
- waterfowl migrate across Saskatchewan in huge numbers each spring and autumn, feeding and resting in wetlands and grainfields
- cold winters, hot summers, low precipitation in plains area; drought and hail can affect crops

## Natural Resources

- agricultural land ideal for growing field crops
- minerals such as potash, salt, uranium and petroleum produced in large quantities; copper, zinc and nickel also found

## Industries and Products

- greatest grower of wheat in North America
- mining and oil

## People and Places

- Regina is the provincial capital, a centre for transportation by road and rail, and a business and government centre.
- Saskatoon is the largest city. It is a service centre for agriculture, nearby potash mines and uranium mines in northern Saskatchewan. The South Saskatchewan River divides the city of Saskatoon in two. Seven bridges connect the two sides of the city.

## Something Special

- All new members of the Royal Canadian Mounted Police (RCMP) receive their training in Regina. The RCMP museum is there.

## Websites

To learn more about Saskatchewan, visit www.gov.sk.ca and www.sasktourism.com

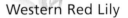

Western Red Lily

Sharp-tailed Grouse

Saskatchewan has been called "Canada's Breadbasket."

Prairie Crocus

Great Grey Owl

Most sunflower seeds are used to produce cooking oil.

# Manitoba

## Fast Facts

- 548 000 square km of land
- 1.1 million people
- Interior Plains, Canadian Shield and Hudson Bay Lowlands regions

Nickname: the Keystone Province

Capital: Winnipeg

Exports: wheat, cereal grains, oil seeds (e.g., sunflower), minerals, electricity, fish, machinery, pulp and paper

Imports: manufactured goods, seafood products

## Environment

- lies in the geographic centre of Canada
- southern Manitoba is flat, low-lying plains; most central and northern parts are in Canadian Shield
- lakes and large rivers cover about one-sixth of Manitoba
- Lake Winnipeg, Canada's fifth largest lake
- tundra in the extreme north: stunted trees, exposed rock and swamps
- Hudson Bay Lowlands region, wetlands and some coniferous forest

## Natural Resources

- minerals: nickel, gold, silver, copper, zinc and lead
- large hydroelectric power plants on the Nelson River
- only tantalum mine in North America at Bernic Lake. Tantalum is used to make chemical process equipment, nuclear reactors, aircraft, and missile parts.
- good agricultural land

## Industries and Products

- wheat, oats and barley
- beef cattle, hogs and poultry raised for food
- other crops include flax, potatoes, sugar beets, sunflowers
- manufacturing: meat products, printed materials, plastic products, farm machinery, trucks, buses and trailers, and dairy products
- transportation and processing centre for farming in the West

## People and Places

- Winnipeg is the provincial capital. It is a centre for grain handling and shipping. The Royal Winnipeg Ballet is a well-known dance company that tours across Canada and elsewhere.
- Portage la Prairie is a smaller city in the heart of the grain-growing belt. It has a museum containing a replica of Fort la Reine. The fort was built by the explorer la Vérendrye when he explored the region.

## Something Special

- A branch of the Royal Canadian Mint is located in Winnipeg. Canadian money and coins are made there.
- Churchill is Canada's most northerly deep-sea port. Visitors from all over the world come to Churchill to visit the world's largest denning area for polar bears.

## Websites

To learn more about Manitoba, visit www.gov.mb.ca and www.travelmanitoba.com

# Nunavut

## Fast Facts

- 2 million square km (land/water)
- 27 000 people
- Arctic Lowlands, Canadian Shield and Hudson Bay Lowlands regions

Nunavut means "our land" in the Inuktitut language of the Inuit

Capital: Iqaluit

Exports: minerals, works of art

Imports: fresh food and dairy products, machinery, manufactured goods

## Environment

- includes seven of Canada's 12 largest islands
- two-thirds of Canada's coastline
- less precipitation in northern area than certain areas of the Sahara Desert
- water frozen much of the year, so plants unable to use it; plants grow very slowly and do not get large
- in places called Barren Lands, plants far apart and rocky earth exposed

## Natural Resources

- no agricultural land and very short growing season; hunting and fishing important for obtaining food
- zinc and lead mined on Little Cornwallis Island and Baffin Island

## Industries and Products

- mining, tourism, fishing, hunting, trapping, arts and crafts production

## People and Places

- Nunavut was once part of the Northwest Territories. It became Canada's third territory April 1, 1999.
- one of the least populated parts of the Earth
- Iqaluit is the territorial capital and the largest community, a centre of government, transportation and business.
- There are more snowmobiles than cars; airplanes are used to transport people, food, machinery and anything else needed in outlying areas.

## Something Special

- Almost every community has an airport or airstrip. There were 16 176 landings and take-offs at Iqaluit Airport in 1997, or 44 a day!

## Websites

To learn more about Nunavut, visit www.gov.nu.ca and www.nunatour.nt.ca and www.arctic-travel.com

Iqaluit is the capital of the newest territory of Canada, Nunavut.

White Trillium

Common Loon

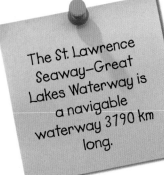

The St. Lawrence Seaway–Great Lakes Waterway is a navigable waterway 3790 km long.

# Ontario

## Fast Facts

- 891 200 square km of land
- 11.5 million people
- Canadian Shield, Hudson Bay Lowlands and St. Lawrence Lowlands regions

Nickname: The Heartland of Canada

Capital: Toronto

Exports: manufactured products, motor vehicles, food and dairy products, minerals, wood, and pulp and paper products

Imports: electricity, oil and gas, seafood

## Environment

- rocks, lakes, rivers and forests of the Canadian Shield cover about half of Ontario
- poor soils and rough landforms made settlement and transportation in the Shield region difficult
- wetlands and coniferous forests of Hudson Bay Lowlands are flat and poorly drained, but provide a home for many animals and birds
- many major river systems
- St. Lawrence Lowlands region has deep fertile soil, mild climate
- the Niagara Escarpment is a limestone ridge running 400 km from Niagara Falls to Manitoulin Island

## Natural Resources

- minerals: iron, copper, lead, nickel, zinc, gold, silver and uranium mined in Canadian Shield area
- petroleum: oil and natural gas found in southwestern Ontario

- forests
  - softwood trees from coniferous forests for pulp and paper
  - deciduous hardwood trees harvested in some areas for building and furniture manufacturing
  - government of Ontario owns 88% of Ontario's forest lands, issues special timber licences to logging companies to harvest trees. Government laws also protect forests because they are valuable for recreation and tourism.
- water
  - many rivers and lakes provide transportation, hydroelectric power and recreational space
  - four of the five Great Lakes lie along the southern border of Ontario; St. Lawrence Seaway connects the St. Lawrence River system to the Great Lakes. This navigable waterway is the cheapest way to transport bulky items like grain, minerals and newsprint.
  - fast-moving rivers and streams are an excellent source of hydroelectric power used by homes and industries
  - cottages and resorts found on many of the 400 000 lakes and rivers
- fertile soil: the small plains area attracted settlers and farmers; today the region contains some of Ontario's largest cities as well as fruit, grain, dairy and mixed farms.

## Industries and Products

- Ontario is the leading manufacturing province in Canada. Automobiles, transportation equipment of all kinds, and computers are just a few examples of the many products made in Ontario.

- agricultural products, including cattle feed, dairy products, meat, vegetables, fruit

- nickel, uranium, copper, gold, zinc and iron produced and exported

- forestry products, including pulp, paper and lumber

- Ontario produces electricity from water, coal, oil and nuclear generators. However, it uses more than it produces, so it must import electricity.

- Financial services and banking are a major industry.

## People and Places

- Ontario is the second largest province in Canada. It has one-third of Canada's population.

- Most of Ontario's population, agriculture and industry are found in the smallest area, part of the St. Lawrence Lowlands region. Over 5 million people live around the western end of Lake Ontario.

- Ottawa is the national capital.

- Toronto is the largest city in Canada by population. In 1998, six boroughs joined together to become a "megacity." There are 4 680 000 people in the Toronto region.

- Toronto is the provincial capital city. It is a centre for business, banking, industry, transportation and technology.

- Many cites in the southeastern area have large manufacturing industries producing products for sale outside the region.

- Other Ontario cities, such as Sault Ste. Marie and Thunder Bay, are mainly involved in transportation and providing services to mining, forestry and people living in the surrounding areas.

Rail lines cross hundreds of kilometres of Canadian Shield to connect Central Canada with Western Canada.

## Something Special

- The main downtown road in Toronto is Yonge Street. This is the longest street in the world.

## Websites

To learn more about Ontario, visit www.gov.on.ca, www.escarpment.org, www.ontariotravel.net and www.tourism.gov.on.ca

Toronto, Ontario, can be easily recognized by the CN Tower, one of the world's largest free-standing structures.

# Map Reading: Boundaries

**Boundaries** are imaginary lines on a globe, road map or atlas. They are used to outline the outside edges of a political region. When they separate two countries, they are called **international boundaries**. These are also called **borders**.

Boundaries also separate political regions within a country. In Canada these are called **provincial** and **territorial boundaries**. They show where one province or territory ends and another begins.

The province of Ontario is divided into districts in the north and counties in the south. **Municipal** boundaries outline areas that have a local government, such as cities, towns and villages.

Detailed maps may show villages, towns and cities. The size of the place is shown by the symbol used. The legend of the map will show you what the symbols stand for.

Southeastern Ontario

LEGEND
- – – International boundary
- – · – Provincial boundary
- – – County boundary

Municipal:
- ☐ City
- ● Town
- ○ Village
- ═══ Major highway
- Heritage park

0    10 km

## Do ◆ Discuss ◆ Discover

1. Examine the map on this page very carefully.

   a) Identify the symbols used for international, provincial and county boundaries. Name examples in your notebook.

   b) Identify the symbols and find examples of a village, a town and a city.

# Quebec

## Fast Facts

- 1.4 million square km of land
- 7.3 million people
- Canadian Shield, Hudson Bay Lowlands, St. Lawrence Lowlands and Appalachian regions

Nickname: *La belle province* (The Beautiful Province)

Capital: Quebec City

Exports: machinery, pulp and paper, minerals, agricultural and food products, electricity, manufactured goods, clothing and textiles

Imports: manufactured goods, oil and gas, wheat

## Environment

- four physical regions: a small area of Hudson Bay Lowlands, a huge area of Canadian Shield, and small areas of the St. Lawrence Lowlands and Appalachian regions

## Natural Resources

- pulp and paper produced from the forests
- hydroelectricity produced along the St. Lawrence, Saguenay, St. Maurice Rivers and La Grande Rivière
- asbestos, gold, iron, copper, silver, zinc, lead and other minerals mined

## Industries and Products

- farming, industry and business in Quebec are centred along the St. Lawrence River
- manufacturing is the most important industry in Quebec; almost one-third of Canadian manufactured products are made in Quebec
- clothing and fabrics, food, paper, metal and wood products
- electricity exported to Ontario, New Brunswick and northeastern United States

## People and Places

- Quebec is the largest province in Canada. In Quebec most people speak French as their first language.
- Most of the population lives in the St. Lawrence Lowlands region; most of Quebec's largest cities are also located there.
- Montreal is the largest city in Quebec. Many companies have their headquarters or head offices situated in Montreal. It is an important business and cultural centre. Montreal was the home of Expo 67 and the 1976 Summer Olympics.
- Quebec City is the provincial capital. It is a historic and beautiful city. It is the sixth largest city in Canada.

## Something Special

- Quebec City has been chosen as a World Heritage Site, so its historic character will be preserved.

## Websites

To learn more about Quebec, visit www.tourisme.gouv.qc.ca and www.quebecregion.com

White Garden Lily

Snowy Owl

Two features of the Quebec Winter Carnival are Le Bonhomme and an ice sculpture competition.

# Newfoundland

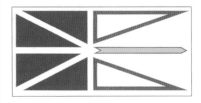

Pitcher Plant

Atlantic Puffin

## Fast Facts

- 371 700 square km of land
- 541 000 people
- Canadian Shield, St. Lawrence Lowlands and Appalachian regions

Nickname: The Rock

Capital: St. John's

Exports: fish and seafood products, petroleum, minerals

Imports: fresh foods, manufactured goods, machinery

## Environment

- the most easterly province in Canada
- two parts: the island of Newfoundland and Labrador on the mainland
- rugged cliffs, mountain ranges, lakes and rivers; 17 000 km of rugged coastline
- most of Labrador is in the Canadian Shield region (a small part of the south coast is part of the St. Lawrence Lowlands)
- island of Newfoundland is part of the Appalachian region
- Continental shelf and Grand Banks off the shore of Newfoundland
- vegetation either coniferous forest or tundra
- sea ice and icebergs move down the coast in the ocean currents
- winter climate is cold and storms frequent

## Natural Resources

- Grand Banks, one of the most important fisheries in the world; fish stocks are in decline
- offshore petroleum being produced at the Hibernia oil field on the Grand Banks
- minerals include gold, iron, nickel, copper, lead, zinc and others
- uranium mined in Labrador and nickel mines being developed at Voisey Bay

## Industries and Products

- manufacturing industry mainly produces fish and forest products
- people of Newfoundland have developed a hand-made craft industry producing souvenirs for the tourism industry

## People and Places

- the last area to become a province of Canada, in 1949
- St. John's is the provincial capital of Newfoundland. It is a port city located near the main shipping lanes of the North Atlantic Ocean and near the Hibernia offshore oil fields. It is North America's oldest city.

## Something Special

- In 1901, an inventor called Guglielmo Marconi received the first wireless message across the Atlantic at Cabot Tower.

## Websites

To learn more about Newfoundland, visit www.gov.nf.ca and www.public.gov.nf.ca/tourism

Cabot Tower on Signal Hill is named after the explorer John Cabot, who arrived in Newfoundland more than 400 hundred years ago.

# New Brunswick

## Fast Facts

- 72 000 square km of land
- 756,600 people
- Appalachian region

Nickname: The Picture Province

Capital: Fredericton

Exports: minerals, pulp and paper, dairy and food products, Christmas trees

Imports: manufactured goods, hydroelectricity, wheat, food products, forest products

## Environment

- Gulf of St. Lawrence lies along the eastern coast; the Bay of Fundy lies between New Brunswick and Nova Scotia
- several important rivers; the longest is the St. John River
- good natural harbours and large forests the basis of shipbuilding industries of the past; ships now built of steel
- tides and ocean currents created unusual shoreline landforms and a number of the tourist sights
- highest tides in the world occur in the Bay of Fundy

## Natural Resources

- mining of zinc and lead, potash, antimony and peat
- forests

## Industries and Products

- mining, forestry, pulp and paper, fishing
- manufacturing of food, textile, wood, paper, metal, chemical and mineral products
- salmon, trout, oysters and mussels raised by aquaculture
- transportation and port services
- new companies produce computer software and other technology products

## People and Places

- One-third of population is francophone, which means they are French-speaking or have French ancestors.
- Moncton nicknamed the Hub of the Maritimes because all railroad lines in the Maritime provinces pass through it.
- Fredericton, located on the St. John River, is the provincial capital. It is a centre of government and education.
- Fredericton is home to the Maritime Forest Ranger School, operated to train forest rangers and technicians.
- Saint John is the largest city in New Brunswick. Canada's largest oil refinery is in Saint John.

Purple Violet

## Something Special

- The Reversing Falls on the Bay of Fundy is one of the marine wonders of the world; the tides push their way against the river current and actually reverse the flow of the rapids. The river runs backwards!

Black-capped Chickadee

## Websites

To learn more about New Brunswick, visit www.gnb.ca and www.travel.org/newbruns.html

The Flowerpot Rocks at Hopewell Cape were created by the action of the sea.

Mayflower

Osprey

# Nova Scotia

## Fast Facts

- 55 500 square km of land
- 940 000 people
- Appalachian region

Nickname: Canada's Ocean Playground

Capital: Halifax

Exports: dairy and food products, fruit, manufactured products (e.g., tires), lumber, Christmas trees, fish and shellfish

Imports: machinery, manufactured products

## Environment

- a **peninsula**, with water on three sides, joined to New Brunswick by a narrow piece of land
- jagged coastline, with nearly 4000 rocky outcroppings and islands
- Cape Breton Island connected to the rest of Nova Scotia by the Canso Causeway
- visited by many migrating birds because roughly halfway between the Equator and the North Pole
- whales found off the coastline of Nova Scotia where fish and seafood are plentiful

## Natural Resources

- softwood and hardwood forests
- coal mining; coal used in generators to provide most of the province's power
- some hydroelectricity
- inshore and offshore fishing
- ice-free deep water harbour at Halifax
- Annapolis Tidal Generating Station uses tides to make electricity
- offshore petroleum fields; new field being developed near Sable Island

## Industries and Products

- dairy and poultry farming; dairy and food products industries
- fruit farming of apples, blueberries and grapes
- fishing and industries such as shipbuilding important during history of Nova Scotia
- pulp and paper industry
- hardwoods for furniture building
- aquaculture produces salmon, lobster, clams and bass
- tourism an important industry

## People and Places

- Most people live close to the sea, in towns and small seaports on sheltered coves and bays.
- Halifax is the provincial capital, a historic port city with a modern, busy international shipping industry.

## Something Special

- The tides in the Bay of Fundy rise higher than a five-story building, up to 16.5 metres in 6 hours. In the village of Bear River, all the buildings are on stilts.

## Webites

To learn more about Nova Scotia, visit www.gov.ns.ca/playground and http://explore.gov.ns.ca

The town of Lunenberg has been named a World Heritage site. It has historical buildings over three hundred years old and a beautiful harbour.

# Prince Edward Island

## Fast Facts

- 5660 square km of land
- 138 000 people
- Appalachian region

Nickname: Garden of the Gulf

Capital: Charlottetown

Exports: farm products, fish, Irish moss (seaweed)

Imports: electricity, manufactured products

## Environment

- the smallest province of Canada, about 230 km long and from 6 to 60 km wide
- almost no inland bodies of fresh water
- highest point on the island, in the Bonshaw Hills, only 142 m above sea level
- fine white beaches on the northern side of the island
- low outcroppings of red sandstone about 6 m high border the southern side

## Natural Resources

- no extensive original forests, but trees grown in woodlots for fuel and some lumber
- good soils and mild climate the basis of the farming industry
- no hydroelectric power; most electricity imported from Nova Scotia by undersea cable
- fish, lobsters and shellfish
- a marine plant, Irish moss, is harvested

## Industries and Products

- farmers raise livestock and grow crops
- potatoes are a major crop
- industries concentrate on farm products and fish
- tourism an important industry

## People and Places

- Charlottetown is the provincial capital city and the Island's largest city. The Charlottetown Conference in 1864 set the stage for the formation of Canada as a nation. Charlottetown is called the "Birthplace of Confederation." It has many tourist visitors.

## Something Special

- Confederation Centre of the Arts has a theatre, museum, art gallery and library. It is the site of the Charlottetown Summer Festival. Each year it produces a musical, Anne of Green Gables, based on the novel by local author Lucy Maud Montgomery.

## Website

To learn more about Prince Edward Island, visit www.gov.pe.ca and www.peisland.com

Lady's Slipper

Blue Jay

When you see reddish coloured rock or soil, there are traces of iron present. It turns the soil the colour of rusty iron.

Fields of potatoes growing in the red soil of Prince Edward Island have given it the name Garden of the Gulf.

# Chapter 9

## Understanding Concepts

1. Following the presentations on the provinces and the territories, work with a partner to develop a comparison chart for any two provinces or territories. (Hints: Compare the province/territory you are focusing on in the Canada Project with one other province or territory. See page 12 for example comparison charts.)

2. Identify vocabulary from this chapter to add to the vocabulary section of your notebook. Draw diagrams or sketches to help you remember the words and their meanings.

3. Create a spelling test for a partner. Include province, territory and capital city names. Give each other a spelling test.

## Developing Inquiry/Research and Communication Skills

4. Draw a poster to encourage visitors to a point of interest, either in Ottawa or any one of the provinces or territories. Include a picture, a slogan, an address, and prices if needed.

## Developing Map/Globe Skills

5. a) Use an atlas and what you have learned about grids to locate the latitude and longitude for your home town or city. Put this in your notebook.

   b) Locate and label your home town or city on the outline map of Canada in your notes.

## Apply Concepts and Skills in Various Contexts

6. Imagine you are visiting Ottawa for a day. You find a Beaver Tail kiosk. Write a story about your day. Illustrate your story.

7. In a small group, use the Ottawa tour map to create new scavenger questions for another group. Use the grid clues to help you form proper clues.

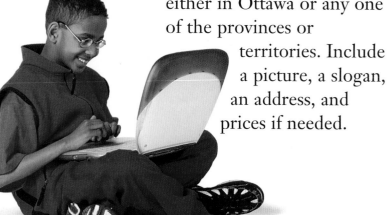

### The Canada Project

Research and create a fact card (like a baseball card) for the capital city and one other city in your province/territory. Remember to put a picture on the front.

# The Canada Project

It is now time for all groups to work on the relief model of Canada. Follow the steps below to build the display.

## Step 1

- In your small group, create an outline of your province or territory on heavy white cardboard. Use an overhead projector to enlarge and trace your part of a map of Canada. Each group needs to use the same base map. That way, all of the provinces and territories will have the same scale and Canada will fit together!

- Use a pencil to sketch the major waterways, landforms and cities onto your province map. Look at the relief map on page 7 (or in your atlas) to figure out the position, shape and elevations of landforms. Your pencil sketch and this information will help at the next stage.

- Carefully cut out the outline of your province or territory.

## Step 2

- As a class, create a continuous sheet of recycled flattened cardboard boxes. You will use it as a base for the final relief model map. Tape the edges of the boxes together and reinforce the joints or seams with extra tape.

- Place your province or territory on the cardboard sheet. (Don't attach it.) Consult with your neighbouring provinces and territories to check that rivers and other features that cross boundaries are correct. Make corrections to your pencil sketch and notes.

## Step 3

- Use modelling dough or clay to create a relief map of your province/territory. Add landforms and bodies of water based on your notes and sketches. Consult with your neighbouring provinces or territories about the elevation of features that cross boundaries. You want the landscape to be continuous.

- Let your relief map dry and then paint it.

- Add labels for landforms, bodies of water, capital cities and other important places.

> **Coming Up**
> Do not glue your province/territory to the cardboard backing yet. You will add more information as you complete the Canada Project.

113

# Chapter 10

# Provincial Government

The people in all of our governments in Canada have been elected to represent us. That means they have been chosen to speak for us and work on our behalf.

An election is an opportunity for people of voting age to choose the people who will represent them. Several candidates compete in each constituency. That is an area that has a representative in government. The elected candidates become the government.

There are three levels of government in Canada: federal, provincial/territorial and municipal.

The federal government is the government of Canada. Elected representatives from every province and territory take part in the federal government.

Provincial and territorial governments are elected by the people of each province and territory. They look after services such as schools, health care and hospitals.

Municipal governments are local governments of towns or cities. They take care of services such as city police and firefighters, local parks and swimming pools.

This chapter will focus on the provincial level of government. It will look at how provincial and territorial governments help the people living in that province or territory.

## Focus on Learning

In this chapter you will learn about
- identifying the parts of a provincial government
- how provincial/territorial governments are elected
- services provided by provincial governments

## Vocabulary

| | | |
|---|---|---|
| election | Judiciary | honourary |
| candidate | premier | political |
| constituency | cabinet | party |
| Executive | minister | commissioner |
| Council | lieutenant- | advance poll |
| Legislative | governor | secret ballot |
| Assembly | | |

# Parts of a Provincial Government

There are three parts of a provincial government. They are the Executive Council, the Legislative Assembly and the Judiciary.

## Executive Council

- also called the Cabinet
- made up of the premier, who is the government leader, and cabinet ministers
- Cabinet ministers are selected from the elected members of government.
- The Executive Council puts forward new laws or changes to laws.

## Legislative Assembly

- made up of all the candidates who were elected in their constituencies
- discusses and makes laws
- sometimes called the legislature or "house"

## Judiciary

- made up of courts and judges
- protects citizens' rights
- interprets and enforces the law

The Legislative Assembly in Ontario has 103 elected representatives called Members of Provincial Parliament, or MPPs.

Each provincial government also has a lieutenant-governor. This position is a tradition from a time in our history when Canada was a colony of Great Britain. The lieutenant-governor is appointed as an honourary head of government. This means that the lieutenant-governor takes part in many ceremonies, but the premier actually leads the government.

The governments of most provinces and territories are made up of Members of the Legislative Assembly, or MLAs.

The Honorable Hilary Weston was appointed the lieutenant-governor of Ontario in 1997.

The provincial premiers sometimes meet to discuss issues. Premier Harris from Ontario is shown here with Premier Klein from Alberta.

## Be a Page!

Each year, boys and girls in Grades 7 and 8 from across Ontario are chosen to be pages in the Ontario Legislative Assembly. The students must have an 80% average in school. Pages deliver messages and run errands for MPPs. They spend four weeks there and receive tutoring to help them keep up with their schoolwork.

# Electing a Provincial Government

A person can vote in a provincial election if they are a Canadian citizen and at least 18 years old. Provincial elections happen at least once every five years.

The candidates that get the most votes from people in their constituency win the election there. They become members of the Legislative Assembly. All the elected members speak for everyone in the province, but especially for the people in their constituency.

Most candidates belong to one of the **political parties**. A political party is a group of people that share common political beliefs. After the election, the political party that had the most candidates elected forms the government. The leader of that political party becomes premier.

## Territorial Government

Territorial governments are very similar to provincial governments. The territories each have a Legislative Assembly made up of representatives elected by the people in the territory. The leader of the Legislative Assembly is called the premier or the government leader.

The federal government appoints a **commissioner** to work with the territorial government. This commissioner is similar to a lieutenant-governor in a province.

Paul Okalik is the first premier of the new territory of Nunavut.

This is the room in the Ontario Legislative Assembly where the government of Ontario meets to discuss and make laws for its citizens.

# Steps in an Election

**1** The provincial government gathers the names of all eligible voters.

**2** The premier meets with the lieutenant-governor to advise him or her that an election is being announced.

**3** Each party announces their candidates for each constituency.

**4** Candidates talk in public about their ideas and say why people should vote for them.

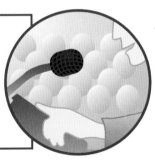

**5** Voters read newspapers, listen to the radio, watch television and go to meetings to become informed about issues. This helps them decide whom to vote for.

**6** If a person cannot vote on election day, he or she votes at an **advance poll** before election day.

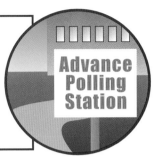

**7** On election day, voters go to a polling station. They are given a **secret ballot** on which to mark their vote. They put an X beside the name of the candidate they choose.

**8** A polling station officer puts each ballot in the ballot box.

**9** The ballots are counted and the results are announced by television, radio and newspapers.

## Do ◆ Discuss ◆ Discover

1. a) As a class, brainstorm ways that you can be involved in an election.

   b) Identify two ways that you think you personally could get involved. Write these in your notebook.

# Government Services

The provincial government has many duties and responsibilities for helping citizens in their day-to-day lives. The web below shows some provincial responsibilities. In some major areas such as health care, responsibility and cost are shared with the federal government.

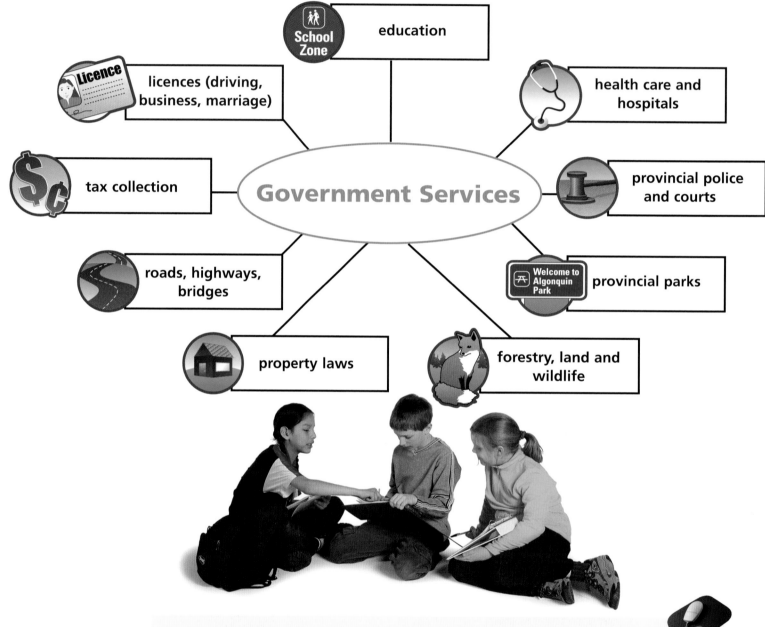

For more information on the Ontario government, go to www.gov.on.ca and click on The Premier's Kid Zone.

## Do ◆ Discuss ◆ Discover

1. Work with a partner to identify four different government services that you use and benefit from. Discuss why these are important to you and what might happen if these services weren't there.

2. If you had to choose the two most important services, what would they be? Explain in a paragraph the reasons for your choices.

# Chapter 10

## Understanding Concepts

1. a) Identify vocabulary from this chapter to add to the vocabulary section of your notebook. Draw diagrams or sketches to help you remember the words and their meanings.

   b) Design five fill-in-the-blanks sentences for the vocabulary words found in this chapter. Exchange your sentences with a partner.

2. a) Create an organizer on provincial and territorial government. On one side of the organizer place your ideas of ways the government is important. Ask your parents or another adult for their ideas of why provincial and territorial governments are important. List their ideas on the other side.

   b) Write three to four summary statements about the information on your organizer.

## Developing Inquiry/Research and Communication Skills

3. Develop three questions you would like to ask your Member of Provincial Parliament if you had the opportunity to interview him/her.

## Developing Map/Globe Skills

4. Research which political party forms the government in each province or territory. On an outline map of Canada, colour each province according to the political party in power. Include a legend.

## Applying Concepts and Skills in Various Contexts

5. Collect a newspaper article on the provincial government. Make point form notes about the topic, information given and people or groups involved. Put these in your notebook.

## The Canada Project

1. Create a political fact sheet about your province/territory. Include the following: Who is the premier? To what political party does he or she belong? Who is the lieutenant-governor or commissioner in your province/territory? What is the legislative assembly called?

2. Try to find a newspaper article and/or photo of an event involving the government of your province/territory.

3. Create a collage of images that show services provided by your provincial/territorial government.

Put all of these in your scrapbook or shoebox.

# Chapter 11
# Connections

## Transportation

## Service Connections

## Connections

## Resources and Products

## Information and Ideas

We have learned that Canada is a large country with many natural differences. Travel and communication are important to Canadians. They connect across the country with each other every day in hundreds of ways.

## Focus on Learning

In this chapter you will learn about
- exchanges that happen between provinces and among the regions
- writing a paragraph
- how the economy in a province or territory and the environment are related
- interviewing for information
- creating maps using symbols for resources and products
- connections among Canadians
- the importance of technology to our lives

## Vocabulary

| | |
|---|---|
| transportation | innovation |
| raw material | services |
| products | public |
| economy | transportation |
| communication | |

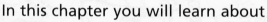

# Transportation

Transportation refers to methods of moving people and goods from one place to another.

Canada has almost 1 000 000 kilometres of highways and 50 000 kilometres of railway tracks. There are 646 certified airports in Canada. There are about 55 ferries that carry passengers, automobiles and freight across bodies of water.

Transportation is one of the most important ways Canadians are connected. People and goods are constantly on the move.

"Trans" means "across." "Port" is the root of a word that means "to carry."

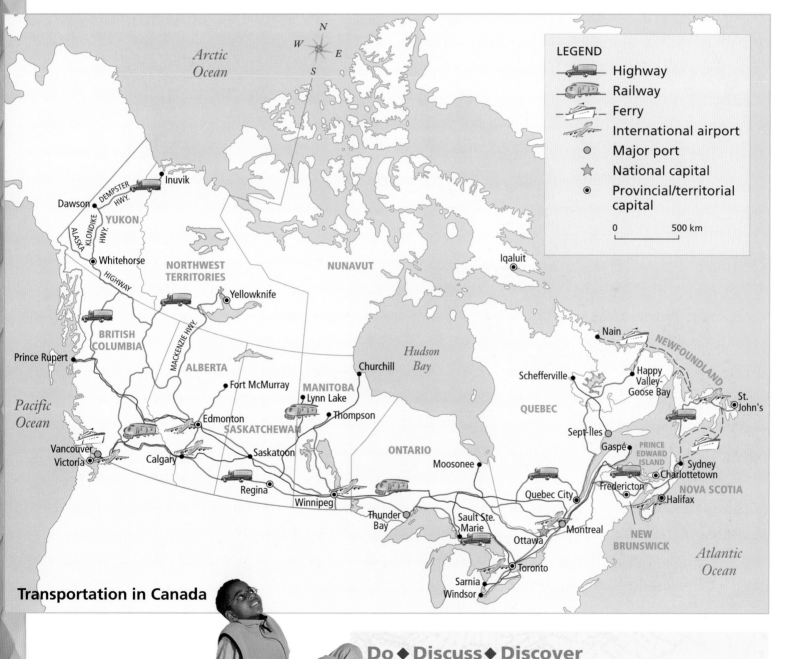

**Transportation in Canada**

## Do ◆ Discuss ◆ Discover

1. On an outline map of Canada, show routes that each of the seven children may have used to get to Ottawa from the different regions of Canada. Use a different colour for each. Put the map in your notebook.

# On the Move

Canadians use many different means of moving people and products. The choice of method is affected by the size and weight of the load, distance to be travelled, barriers to travel, and the speed required.

## Other Ways of Moving Things

Information and energy are also carried or sent to others across the country and around the world. Some methods used are

- fibre-optic cable
- satellites
- radio waves
- telephone lines
- power lines
- pipelines

### Do ◆ Discuss ◆ Discover

1. a) Review pages 121 and 122 and work in small groups to brainstorm examples of land, water and air transportation. Give two examples of materials or products that could be transported by each method.
   b) As a class, share your ideas and create a master list of the types of transportation on chart paper. Post it on the wall in your classroom.

# Writing a Paragraph

Good paragraphs have three parts:

1.  The first sentence tells what the paragraph will be about.

2.  The sentences in the middle give more information about the topic.

3.  The last sentence finishes the paragraph with an interesting comment about the topic.

There are three steps to writing a paragraph:

1.  Develop an idea about the topic. One good way is to create a web of facts you know about the topic. Here is an example:

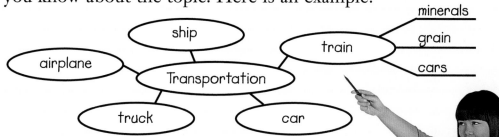

2.  Plan your paragraph using the information from the idea web.

    *   What will you say about the topic in your opening sentence?

    *   What will you say about each supporting idea in the middle sentences?

    *   What is the best order to put them in?

    *   What will your closing sentence say about the topic?

3.  Use the plan to write your paragraph.

4.  Reread your paragraph and correct any errors. Write out your final, finished copy.

**Do ◆ Discuss ◆ Discover**

Choose either number 1 or 2:

1.  Look back at the map you did on page 121. Choose one of the seven children who came to Ottawa. Write a paragraph about his or her journey to Ottawa for the conference. What forms of transportation did they use? In what sequence did they use them?

2.  Write a paragraph about a trip you have taken and the forms of transportation you used. Describe where you went, and include something interesting and fun that you did.

# From Harvest to Sale

Transportation of goods occurs many times between harvesting a resource and selling a finished product made from the **raw material**. The diagrams below show two sequences from harvest to sale.

**Making Breakfast Cereal**

**Making a Cereal Package**

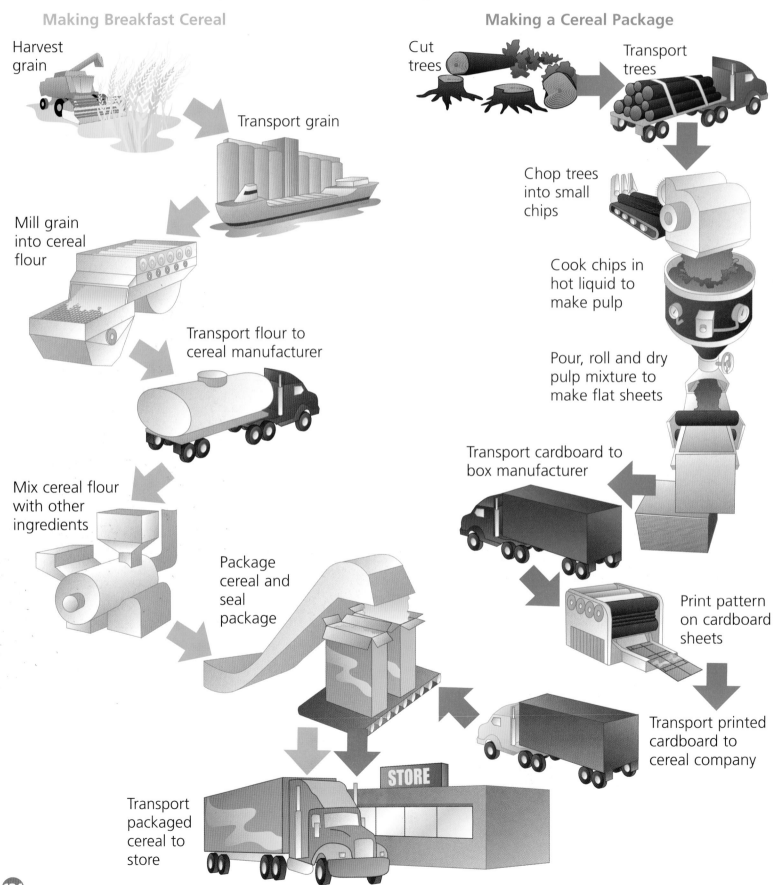

Harvest grain

Transport grain

Mill grain into cereal flour

Transport flour to cereal manufacturer

Mix cereal flour with other ingredients

Package cereal and seal package

Cut trees

Transport trees

Chop trees into small chips

Cook chips in hot liquid to make pulp

Pour, roll and dry pulp mixture to make flat sheets

Transport cardboard to box manufacturer

Print pattern on cardboard sheets

Transport printed cardboard to cereal company

Transport packaged cereal to store

STORE

# Resources and Products

Manufacturing industries turn raw materials into products. Some industries process or refine raw materials. That means they change them into a different, more useful state. For example, a smelter processes raw iron ore into pure iron.

Other industries turn processed materials into final **products**. For example, cars are manufactured from many different parts. Metal, plastic, rubber, glass and other types of parts are assembled into a final product.

In the photos on this page, workers are involved in the food industry, the clothing industry, the auto industry and the high-tech industry (computer hardware).

The provinces and territories of Canada buy and sell resources and products to and from each other and places outside Canada. The **economy** is based on exchange.

If a place has many resources or if it manufactures many products that other places wish to buy, it will have a strong economy.

## Do ◆ Discuss ◆ Discover

1. In groups of three, brainstorm as many ideas as you can of examples of industries. Share your ideas with another group and make any changes or corrections necessary. Put these lists in your notebook.

# Shopping Day

**Food Products**

Breakfast CEREAL

MILK

GRAPE JUICE

MAPLE SYRUP

LEAN

Steak

**Other Products**

Daily News
This Just In!

Motor Oil

Plastic Garbage Bags

Peat Moss

1¢ $1 25¢
$2 5¢ 1¢ 10¢
10¢ 25¢ 5¢ 1¢ 1¢

## Do ◆ Discuss ◆ Discover

1. In groups of three, choose four products from the items above. Discuss the following questions. Write out your notes and put them in your notebook.

   a) Discuss where in Canada the products on this page might have come from. Remember that some products have several different parts. Where would the different parts have come from?

   b) Discuss what kind of packaging each of the items would have. Where did the packaging come from?

   c) Energy was used to make and transport all of these projects. What types of energy might have been used? Where might it come from?

# Interviewing

An interview is a conversation conducted to gather information. The information may be written down or recorded on tape with the person's permission. Use the following as a guide for interviewing:

- Consider your topic and think of questions for which you would like answers. Key questions for gaining information often begin with who, what, where, when, how and why.
- You are the interviewer. Pick a person who has information that you would like to learn. This is your interviewee. If you do not know much about the person or the topic, do background research before you begin.
- Write the questions you are going to ask on a piece of paper. Leave lots of space between questions to write down his or her answers in point form.
- Work with a parent or teacher to arrange a time and a place for the interview. Explain the purpose of the interview to the interviewee. You may want to use a tape recorder as well as take notes by hand. Ask permission to record on tape.
- Record the interviewee's answers. If a person gives an incomplete answer, always ask a follow-up question so you get the information you need.
- At the end of the session, thank the person. Immediately write out your notes of the answers before you forget what you were told.
- Write up the interview using a format like this:

  Interviewer: "Do you like what you do?"
  Interviewee: "Yes, but it is hard work with long hours."

- Give a copy of the interview to the interviewee. People like to read their answers to your questions. This also gives them a chance to correct any errors in your notes or give you more information.

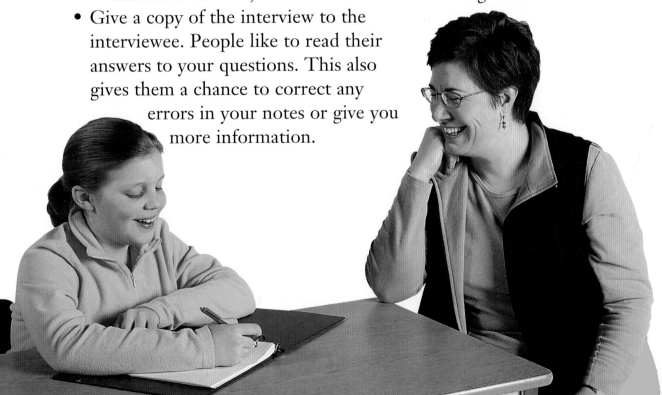

# Information and Ideas

Canadians are connected by the ways they exchange information and ideas with others. This is called **communication**.

There are many ways to communicate ideas and connect with other people.

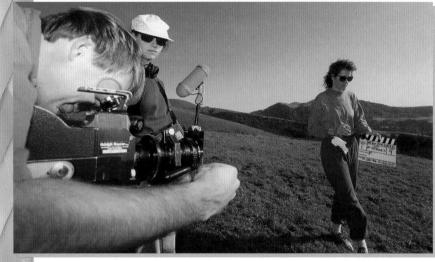

Radio and television and movies are ways of sharing information, ideas and entertainment. We hear the voices and see the faces of many Canadians on television.

National newspapers and magazines let people know what is happening all across the country.

Sports teams like the Toronto Raptors travel across Canada and to other countries to compete with others. We may watch them on television or travel to see them play.

©2001 NBA Entertainment. Photo by Ron Turenne.

Musicians and songwriters create recordings played by people across Canada. Award-winning Canadian performers like Shania Twain represent Canada to people in other countries.

Many authors have created books that show Canada to others. This house was the setting for Anne of Green Gables, by Lucy Maud Montgomery.

Visual artists communicate ideas in paintings, drawings, sculptures and mixed media objects.

Many special schools like the National Ballet School in Toronto have students from all over the country.

Canadian athletes take part in competitions in Canada and in other countries. Champions like gold-medalist Daniel Igali represent Canada in Olympic Games.

The Internet and e-mail are two new ways to share information and ideas with people all over the world.

## Do ◆ Discuss ◆ Discover

1. Review the Interviewing section on page 127. Interview one of your parents or another adult.
   - What job do they do?
   - What are two forms of communication they use in their work?
   - Do these forms of communication help make their work easier? If yes, how?
   - What is the main kind of information or ideas they communicate to other Canadians?

   Share the responses with one other student and put them in your notebook.

2. As a class, create a large group poster called Communicating in Canada. Each student provides one example of an image of a person or event to put on it. Put the poster up in your classroom.

# Innovations

An **innovation** is something that is new. Innovations include discovering something that exists but isn't known about, or inventing something new that did not exist before.

Some Canadians are well-known because they have invented or discovered something that makes life better for others. Other Canadian inventors are less well-known, but their innovations are used and valued by many.

Joseph-Armand Bombardier invented the snowmobile. In northern areas of Canada, in many cases, the snowmobile has taken the place of dogsleds.

The discovery of insulin by Sir Frederick Banting and Charles Best has allowed diabetics to live a healthier life.

James Naismith invented a game for his students using a ball and two peach baskets, which developed into the game of basketball.

The International Space Station project uses the Canadarm for building and repairing the space station.

## Do ◆ Discuss ◆ Discover

1. a) In small groups, discuss why each of the innovations/inventions on this page is important.
   b) Create a chart to show the original problem, the solution provided by the inventor, and a few sentences telling how the invention has changed the lives of those who use it. Put this chart in your notebook.

# Service Connections

Services are groups or individuals who do something that someone needs. There are many kinds of services. They often supply people with special knowledge, skills and sometimes equipment.

Not every community can meet the needs of all of the people all of the time. Some services are only needed occasionally. Often people must come from another community or region to provide the service. This is one way Canadians form connections with each other.

Internet companies and ambulances are examples of service industries.

Most of the banks in Canada have branches all across the country. They assist businesses and individuals with financial help.

People in small, isolated communities may be visited by doctors or nurses at certain regular times. In an emergency, either a doctor flies to see them or they are flown to see the doctor!

The Royal Canadian Mounted Police enforce laws that protect all Canadians. RCMP officers work in all parts of the country.

Industries that are far from cities sometimes need special services. Inspectors travel from one pipeline site to another to check that work is being done safely.

Public transportation includes all of the ways that we pay to ride someplace. People who work on airplanes, buses, trains and ferries help us get where we are going in Canada.

Many people are employed in tourism, making other people's vacations fun, safe and comfortable. This visitor is being welcomed by a worker at the Canadian National Exhibition.

Sometimes there is an emergency in a community that affects many people and causes a lot of damage. The Canadian Armed Forces sometimes help in emergencies and disasters.

## Do ◆ Discuss ◆ Discover

1. a) As a class, discuss how people provide services that connect Canadians.
   b) Take a walk through your neighbourhood. Look for information about services to the community. Discuss services in your community in your class, and then write two or three paragraphs about your discussion. Put this in your notebook.

# Chapter 11

## Understanding Concepts

1. Identify vocabulary from this chapter to add to the vocabulary section of your notebook. Draw diagrams or sketches to help you remember the words and their meanings.

2. Identify and list one example of a connection between provinces/territories in the following categories: transportation, resources and products, information and ideas, and service connections.

3. Explain in point form notes how the different types of landforms and bodies of water in Canada create challenges for providing services, transporting goods and communication.

## Developing Map/Globe Skills

4. With a partner, sketch a map of your neighbourhood. Label the service connections that you have found (for example, doctor, dentist, post office, bank, hospital, lawyer, plumber, police station). Remember to use symbols, colour and a legend to show roads and places on the map.

## Applying Concepts and Skills in Various Contexts

5. In paragraphs, identify and explain how four of the inventions below have made life for people in Canada easier or better.

| | | |
|---|---|---|
| snowmobile | garbage bag | frozen food |
| snowblower | lacrosse | insulin |
| McIntosh apple | snowplow | zipper |
| pablum | telephone | basketball |

## The Canada Project

Each group will now continue work on the relief model of Canada that you started at the end of Chapter 9.

### Step 1

- In your small group, identify the major natural resources and products produced in your province/territory. Refer to your completed map of Canada that you worked on throughout Chapters 2 to 8 for information.

- Make symbols for each natural resource and product. Attach them to your province/territory model.

### Step 2

- Use a pencil to sketch the major transportation routes (rail, highway, pipelines) in your province/territory. Look at the map on page 121 for help. Consult with your neighbouring provinces/territories to make sure the routes cross boundaries correctly. Make corrections to your pencil marks.

- Use different colours of marker pens to carefully mark the pencilled transportation routes in your province/territory. Cooperate with the other students to choose a single system of colours for different types of routes.

# The Canada Project
# Finishing Touches

## The Relief Model

- Work together as each group carefully attaches its province/territory model to the cardboard base to create the relief model of Canada.

- Identify three resources or products that your province or territory exports to another province or territory.

- Use a variety of coloured ribbons or strings to show these exchanges in Canada. Run ribbons or strings from three symbols in your province/territory to provinces/territories that import them. Attach the ribbons or strings onto the relief model using pins or glue.

## Focus Questions

- How is your province/territory important to the whole of Canada?

- How is the rest of Canada important to your province/territory?

- What is special about your province/territory?

## Let's Meet and Talk about Connections

1. Each group will present its province/territory to the class. Be sure to include the following:

   a) Give an interesting and fun introduction to your province or territory. This could be a television commercial, poem, mime, skit, puppet show or song. Make sure everyone in your group takes part.

   b) Present your shoebox and scrapbook. Display the contents of the shoebox, explaining each item. Do the same for the items in the scrapbook. Each person in the group should speak as well as help create the display. Remember to refer to the relief model during your presentation.

2. In Chapters 2 to 8, the seven children each presented a concern in their region, which you have discussed. Each group will now present one of the concerns that is important in its province/territory. If your province/territory is part of more than one region, choose only one of the concerns to present.

   a) Consider the following:
      • Clearly identify the concern.
      • Develop a slogan to bring the issue to people's attention.
      • What solutions or actions do you suggest?
      • How can people in other regions help each other?

   b) Ask the audience if they have any questions. Answer all the questions as best you can.

Share the work you have done and enjoy yourselves!

# Glossary

## A

**acid rain**—precipitation mixed with harmful chemicals, which damages things it falls on

**adaptation**—special features of an animal or plant that help it survive; for example, the Arctic hare grows white fur in the winter, which makes it difficult for predators to see

**advance poll**—place to vote before election day

**animal life**—the animals, birds, fish and other living creatures of an area

**aquaculture**—the business of raising fish or shellfish as a crop to be harvested; similar to agriculture

**Arctic Circle**—an imaginary line around the Earth located at 63½° North latitude

## B

**badlands**—dry lands where the rocks have been worn into unusual shapes by erosion, as in southeastern Alberta

**ballot**—the piece of paper marked by a voter to elect a candidate in an election

**bar graph**—a visual way of showing numerical (number) information; the amounts are shown as bars and measured on a scale marked in units

**barren**—an area of land with almost no living plants

**border**—a boundary; a line on a map separating two political regions

**boundary**—a border, or a line that outlines a political region such as a country, province or territory

**breed**—the act of creating young

## C

**cabinet minister**—person chosen by the premier to be one of his/her advisors and to be head of a government department

**canal**—a narrow channel dug to carry a stream of water, used for transportation or irrigation

**candidate**—a person who chooses to run for election

**capital city**—the city where the government of a country, province or territory meets

**cardinal directions**—the four main directions on a compass: North, East, South, and West

**carnivore**—a meat-eating animal

**cartographer**—a person who draws maps and charts

**chart**—an organized way of showing information

**climate**—the pattern of average temperature and precipitation of a place over a long period of time

**commercial**—selling goods or services

**commissioner**—the representative of the federal government in a territorial government

**communication**—exchanging information and ideas with others

**comparison chart**—an organizer that shows how two or more things are the same and how they are different

**compass rose**—an illustration on a map that shows the directions

**coniferous**—trees with needles and cones; sometimes called evergreens

**conservation**—taking good care of our environment

**constituency**—a specific area from which representatives are elected, also called ridings

**continental shelf**—an area where the ocean floor slants downward gradually for many kilometres and then suddenly drops off into a deep trench

**criteria**—important characteristics of something, used in making comparisons

**cross-section**—a drawing of a slice through something that shows how it looks inside

## D

**deciduous**—trees that lose their leaves each year and grow new leaves the next season

**delta**—an area of flat land at the mouth of a river, often shaped like a triangle. Several branches of the river may flow through it to the ocean.

**dormant**—waiting or sleeping; some plants become brown and wait for rain before they put out new green shoots

**drought**—a long time without precipitation

## E

**economy**—the wealth and resources of a place

**eco-tourism**—people travelling to a place to see the animals, vegetation and landforms in their natural state

**election**—the process in which people vote for a person to be their representative in government

**elevation**—the height of land above or below sea level, usually measured in metres

**environment**—our surroundings; the air, the land and the water around us

**erosion**—natural forces such as wind and water wearing away landforms and carrying the particles away

**escarpment**—a long rock cliff where the elevation of land changes abruptly

**estuary**—the wide mouth of a river, where the flow of the river water is affected by ocean tides

**Executive Council**—the part of the provincial government that includes the premier and cabinet, which puts forward laws to be voted on

## F

**federal**—having to do with the central government for a country

**federal government**—the central government of a country

**fertile**—the ability of soil to produce healthy plants and crops

## G

**gale**—a strong windstorm

**geographer**—a person who studies the surface of the Earth and the effects of human activity on the environment

**glacier**—a huge mass of ice hundreds of metres deep that grows or shrinks as climate changes

**government**—the group of people in a country, province or city that makes and enforces laws for its citizens

**Grand Banks**—an area on the continental shelf southeast of Newfoundland that is world famous for fishing

**graph**—a visual way of organizing and showing numerical (number) information

**grid**—a pattern of regularly spaced lines forming squares, used to locate information on maps; lines of latitude and longitude

## H

**habitat**—the natural home of an animal or plant

**hardwood**—lumber made from the hard-to-cut wood of broad-leafed trees like maple or oak

**harvest**—to collect a crop or resource

**herbivore**—a plant-eating animal

**honourary**—given a title, respect and recognition, but holding little real power

**humidity**—the amount of water vapour in the air

**hydroelectricity**—electricity produced by the force of water

## I, J

**Ice Age**—a period of time hundreds of thousands of years ago when most of Canada was covered with glaciers and the temperatures of the Earth were much lower. During the Ice Ages, glaciers grew and flowed down over North America.

**images**—sources of visual information such as photographs, paintings, drawings and sculptures

**industry**—a business that collects raw materials, creates products for sale or provides services

**innovation**—something that is new; a new way of doing something, a discovery or invention of something new

**inshore fishing**—fishing near the shoreline, not in the open ocean; usually a small or family-run business of catching fish

**intermediate directions**—the directions between the main four directions; for example, North-East

**irrigation**—a method of bringing water to crops

**Judiciary**—the part of the provincial government that interprets and enforces the laws; made up of courts and judges

## L

**landforms**—natural features of the Earth such as mountains, hills, plateaus and plains

**latitude**—imaginary lines that run around the Earth parallel to the Equator. They are used to locate places on the Earth and measure distances north and south of the Equator.

**legend**—a list showing the meanings of symbols, colours and lines used on a map

**Legislative Assembly**—the part of the provincial government that discusses, debates and makes laws; made up of candidates who won an election in their constituency

**lieutenant-governor**—the representative of the Queen in a provincial government, who opens and closes the legislature and signs papers as they become laws

**locks**—structures on a waterway used to raise and lower boats in places where the elevation changes greatly

**longitude**—imaginary lines that reach from the North Pole to the South Pole. Lines of longitude are used to locate places and time zones on the Earth.

## M

**magma**—molten rock under the Earth's crust. Igneous rock is formed when magma cools.

**map**—a drawing or diagram of part of the Earth's surface seen from above

**meteorite**—a rock that comes crashing to Earth from outer space

**mouth**—(of a river) the place where a river empties into an ocean or large body of water

**municipal**—having to do with the local government of a town, city, county or district

**muskeg**—an area of boggy, wet ground and decaying plants

## N

**natural resources**—materials found in nature that are used by people to make life easier and more enjoyable; for example, forests, water and minerals

**non-renewable resources**—natural resources that disappear after being used; for example, gold and oil

## O

**ocean current**—a stream of moving water within a larger body of water

**offshore fishing**—fishing in the open ocean far from the shore. Large ships that can process the fish at sea are common.

**organizer**—a chart that helps show how information is related

**outcrop**—bedrock that is visible through the soil

## P

**peat**—a deep layer of decaying plant life formed in wet conditions

**peninsula**—a piece of land surrounded on three sides by water

**permafrost**—ground that remains frozen all year round

**physical features**—the landforms, rivers and lakes found in the area

**physical region**—an area that has similar physical characteristics throughout, such as landforms, climate, vegetation and resources

**picture graph**—a visual way of organizing numerical (number) information. A legend is provided to show the amount each picture represents.

**pingos**—rounded hills with a core of solid ice found in areas with permafrost

**political party**—a group of people who share common beliefs about government

**political region**—a place or area that has an agreed-upon boundary and its own government

**precipitation**—moisture that falls in the form of rain, snow, sleet or hail, measured as centimetres of water

**predator**—an animal that kills other animals for food

**premier**—the leader of the political party that won the most seats in the legislative assembly; leader of a provincial or territorial government

**products**—items that have been created by industries

**province**—a major political division in Canada

**provincial**—having to do with a major political region within a country

**public transportation**—all of the ways to travel someplace that people pay to use in groups (not their own automobile)

**R**

**raw materials**—natural resources that are processed or refined by industries; industries change the natural resources into a different, more useful state

**region**—an area that is similar throughout and different from the places around it

**relief map**—a map that uses colour to represent elevation and show what the surface of the land is like; it may use some symbols

**renewable resources**—natural resources that do not disappear after being used because more are produced; for example forests

**represent**—stand in the place of someone or something

**river system**—all the parts of a river and its tributaries

**S**

**satellite image**—image of the Earth's surface created from information gathered and recorded by a satellite in orbit

**scale**—the relationship between distance measured on a map and the real distance on the Earth's surface

**sea ice**—ice formed in the salt water of oceans, seas and straits

**sea level**—the average level of the ocean's surface, used as a base to measure the heights of landforms

**secret ballot**—each voter marks a ballot privately and no one can look at the ballot before it goes into the ballot box

**sediment**—particles of sand, soil and other material that drop to the bottom of a river or body of water

**sedimentary rock**—rock made from many layers of sediment that settled on top of each other and, over time, hardened into stone

**services**—groups or individuals who do something that is needed by others

**softwood**—the easy-to-cut wood of a coniferous tree

**source**—the place at which a river begins; for example, a lake, an underground spring or a melting glacier

**statistics**—a collection of facts about people and places shown in numbers

**strait**—a narrow passage of water connecting two larger bodies of water

**symbol**—something that stands for or represents something else

**T**

**territorial**—having to do with a territory

**territory**—a political region not yet a province, where control is shared between the territorial and the federal governments

**theory**—an idea that scientists believe to be true because there is a great deal of evidence, but it has not been proven

**tidal range**—the difference between the water level at high tide and low tide

**tides**—changes in the level of the water that are caused by the pull of the moon's gravity

**transportation**—moving people and goods from one place to another

**trawler**—a big fishing boat that pulls nets or lines through the ocean to harvest fish in large numbers

**treeline**—an imaginary line beyond which trees can no longer grow; for example, trees cannot grow high on mountain tops or in the far North

**tributary**—a creek, stream or river that flows into a larger river

**tundra**—large areas of treeless plain in the far North; tundra vegetation includes low shrubs, small plants and mosses

**V, W**

**vegetation**—the plants that naturally grow in a region

**Venn diagram**—an organizer used to compare ways things are the same and different

**wetlands**—lands that are covered with water all or most of the time

# Index

Arctic Ocean

N
W E
S

Pacific Ocean

YUKON

NORTHWEST TERRITORIES

NUNA

BRITISH COLUMBIA

ALBERTA

SASKATCHEWAN

MANITOBA

Canada